1

WITHDRAWN

3/08

I.C.C. LIBRARY

Also by Molly Ivins and Lou Dubose

Bushwhacked: Life in George W. Bush's America

Shrub: The Short but Happy Political Life of George W. Bush

Also by Molly Ivins

Who Let the Dogs In? Incredible Political Animals I Have Known

You Got to Dance with Them What Brung You: Politics in the Clinton Years

Nothin' but Good Times Ahead

Molly Ivins Can't Say That, Can She?

Also by Lou Dubose

Vice: Dick Cheney and the Hijacking of the American Presidency (with Jake Bernstein)

The Hammer: Tom DeLay, God, Money, and the Rise of the Republican Congress (with Jan Reid)

Boy Genius: Karl Rove, the Brains Behind the Remarkable Political Triumph of George W. Bush (with Jan Reid and Carl M. Cannon)

BILL OF WRONGS

BILL OF WRONGS

THE EXECUTIVE BRANCH'S ASSAULT ON AMERICA'S FUNDAMENTAL RIGHTS

MOLLY IVINS
AND LOU DUBOSE

I.C.C. LIBRARY

RANDOM HOUSE NEW YORK

JC
599
.U5
I85
2007

Copyright © 2007 by Lou Dubose and The Estate of Molly Ivins

All rights reserved.

Published in the United States by Random House,
an imprint of The Random House Publishing Group,
a division of Random House, Inc., New York.

Random House and colophon are registered trademarks of
Random House, Inc.

Library of Congress Cataloging-in-Publication Data

Ivins, Molly.
Bill of wrongs: the executive branch's assault on America's
fundamental rights / Molly Ivins and Lou Dubose.
p. cm.
ISBN: 978-1-4000-6286-7
1. Civil rights—United States. 2. United States. Constitution.
1st–10th Amendments. 3. Executive power—United States.
I. Dubose, Lou. II. Title.
JC599.U5I85 2007
323.4'90973—dc22 2007025724

Printed in the United States of America on acid-free paper

www.atrandom.com

2 4 6 8 9 7 5 3 1

First Edition

Book design by Susan Turner

11/07 B&T 24.95

To Audre and Bernard Rapoport, of Waco, Texas, who are a public good and generous supporters of The Texas Observer, *where both authors began their careers*

CONTENTS

INTRODUCTION

A Republic—If We Can Keep It

To those who scare peace-loving people with phantoms of lost liberty, my message is this: Your tactics only aid terrorists; for they erode our national unity and diminish our resolve. They give ammunition to America's enemies, and pause to America's friends.

—Attorney General John Ashcroft, December 5, 2001

I set out to write this book as a cheerful and joyous tribute to all the heroes I have met over all the years, the folks who make the Bill of Rights more than just dead words on an old parchment. They make those rights into living, breathing freedom. I wanted to write this book because I believe every generation of Americans has to work to "keep it," as Mr. Franklin said of our republic.

I wanted to tell the stories of the contemporary heroes—plain, average, normal, everyday Americans—who stand up for freedom, even when it pisses off their neighbors and costs them a lot, one way or another.

This book grows out of a long-standing commitment of mine. For more than fifteen years, I have made at least one free speech a month on behalf of the Bill of Rights. I started doing the speeches because of a promise I made to a dying friend: How's that for touching?

Actually, it was ridiculous: I promised John Henry Faulk I would take care of the First Amendment, a fairly ludicrous case of overreach. John Henry Faulk was a Texas folklorist, humorist, and the man who broke the blacklisting system in radio and television. When Johnny got blacklisted in 1956—for being a "premature anti-Fascist" (he never did like Hitler)—he did not go gently into that dark night. Instead, he promptly sued the sons of bitches. It's a fine story—Edward R. Murrow took out a mortgage on his house to pay John Henry's lawyer, Louis Nizer, one of the great trial attorneys of the day. The blacklisters were represented by one Roy Cohn. Murray Kempton's hilarious account of the proceedings is worth looking up. Of course it all took years to come to trial, by which time Johnny was not only out of showbiz but totally broke. For the remaining years of his life, he made a slim living as an after-dinner speaker, telling his stories of great Texas characters, but far more important, he functioned as a friend of the First Amendment—anywhere, everywhere, all the time—funny, irreverent, and in love with Jefferson and Madison.

The only time I have ever broken what I consider my commitment to John Henry—one free speech a month someplace where it's needed—was while writing this book. Through two rounds with breast cancer, and some subsequent heart problems, not to mention many a massive hangover, I have staggered onto a plane and arrived at Lard Lake or Fluterville, where some desperate citizens needed help. I've made a locally adapted variation of my basic speech, which includes some great stories and, if I do say so myself, is actually fairly funny.

I began doing this under the illusion that I was being noble and self-sacrificing—not that I would toot my own horn, but I kind of hoped others might notice what a commendable citizen I am. As so often happens when we give to others, the speech a month became not a sacrifice but a continuing source of inspiration, courage, and energy. The commitment hasn't so much cost me time and effort as it has repaid me tenfold by letting me get to know the real heroes of freedom in this country: I have received so much more than I have ever given to this cause; I have been enriched beyond my ability to describe.

My deal with all the First Amendment groups is that I do not give my speech in New York City or San Francisco. I usually do not go anywhere there are a lot of liberals. Consequently, I have spent a lot of time in small cities and towns in Mississippi, northern Georgia, Alabama, northern Louisiana, north Florida, odd parts of the Carolinas, the Dakotas, western Michigan, Utah, Nebraska, Idaho, Montana, Kansas, and Oklahoma. I say unto you, you do not know what courage is until you have sat in the basement of a Holiday Inn in Fritters, Alabama, with seven brave souls, led by a librarian, who are fixing to form a chapter of the Ay Cee Ell You. They are always driven to this extreme by local pinheads who not only don't get the Bill of Rights but are eager to trash it.

I have been called in through the American Library Association on some bizarre cases: say, the local Christian fundamentalists have decided talking animals are satanic, and consequently, they demand *The Three Little Pigs*, *Goldilocks and the Three Bears*, and *The Wind in the Willows* be removed from the town library. Town meeting to be held, can I come and explain the First Amendment?

I try to explain what the First Amendment means with good stories, because that's what John Henry taught me to do. For that matter, Mark Twain and Jesus were both fond of the form, not that I'm putting myself anywhere near there. You'd be amazed at how much even the most sophisticated people still enjoy a good story. And you will find a lot of good stories in this book.

Reporting and telling these stories with me is my colleague Lou Dubose. We have done two books together: *Shrub: The Short but Happy Political Life of George W. Bush* (describing George Bush's failed oil career and disastrous six years as governor of our state) and *Bushwhacked: Life in George W. Bush's America* (for anyone who didn't heed our warning the first time). Lou has also written books on Karl Rove, Tom DeLay, and Dick Cheney. Some people know how to amuse themselves.

I started with the First Amendment for obvious reasons—if you're a journalist, freedom of speech and freedom of the press are matters of both personal and professional self-interest. Over the years, I have of necessity spent more and more time on the very first sixteen words of the First Amendment, which establish the most important right of all: freedom of conscience. Also known as the Establishment Clause. This includes the newly controversial concept of separation of church and state. In addition, I have found myself involved in several controversies involving the other nine of the original ten amendments that form the Bill of Rights.

I meant for this to be a hopeful and a gladsome romp through some serious terrain, and I do think the book includes some right joyous tales. To all the daring, courageous, or just plain stubborn "ordinary" Americans who have ever gotten up on their hind legs and said, "Well, that's not right, that's not fair": this book is still dedicated to you.

But since September 11, 2001, the story of those who stand up for American freedom has gotten darker. The extraordinary heroes are still out there, but now we find more victims of our failure to stand up for our own rights. Their stories start like Kafka's *The Trial.*

> "But how can I be under arrest? And how come it's like this?" "Now you're starting again," said the policeman. . . . "We don't answer questions like that." "You will have to answer

> them," said K. "Here are my identification papers, now show me yours and I certainly want to see the arrest warrant." "Oh, my God!" said the policeman. "In a position like yours, and you think you can start giving orders, do you?"

As much as those victims kick back when their constitutional rights are trampled by their government, it keeps happening, stranger and stranger, creepier and creepier. But of course we must not scare Americans with phantoms of lost liberty: that would be helping the terrorists. But as Pastor Martin Niemöller reminded us when Hitler started locking people up, we all can be suspects in the end: "First they came for the Communists, and I didn't speak up because I wasn't a Communist. Then they came for the Jews, and I didn't speak up because I wasn't a Jew. Then they came for the Catholics, and I didn't speak up because I was Protestant. Then they came for me, and by that time there was no one left to speak for me."

Most Americans still believe this secret-police, secret-detention stuff applies only to foreigners, to illegals, to resident aliens—to people who are not "real citizens." No one likes the messenger who brings the bad news, but pay attention, Americans: *Your ass is on the line.* And so we have included in this book some genuinely dismaying stories.

As one who prefers the funny side of our political life, I have derived considerable amusement over the years from poking fun at the eternally earnest liberals who hear the sound of jackbooted fascism around every corner. Liberals have used the F-word promiscuously, not just in such hair-raising episodes as the Saturday Night Massacre under Richard Nixon but also in completely dipshit cases.

As a Texas liberal, I have developed a positively British case of phlegm. According to medieval medicine, "phlegm" is one of the four "humours," and it accounts for those of us who are hard to startle. If ever there was a group that knew how to survive political reverses, your Texas liberals are the past masters. I do not discombobulate easily. Experience has taught me that things are likely to get worse, so these will eventually turn out to be the Good Old Days, and think what a fool you'll feel like later if you don't enjoy them now.

So please, weigh into this claim my forty years of bearing with perpetually awful political news. Now, as the man said, "My hair is on fire." I am so freaked out about what is happening to freedom in this country, if I were anyone else but me, I'd be staging a pitched, shrieking, quivering, hysterical, rolling-on-the-ground, speaking-in-tongues fit.

Fortunately for you, I have phlegm. Instead of a pitched fit, I have stories to tell, each of them about "an ordinary, certifiably normal" human bean. Too many of whom have blundered into a "phantom of lost liberty."

This has happened before in our history—in fact, it's a pretty predictable reaction to fear. We get so rattled by some Big Scary Thing—communism or crime or drugs or illegal aliens or terrorism—something that scares us so much, we think we can make ourselves safer by giving up some of our freedom. Now, not only does that not hold a drop of water as a logical proposition but it has consistently proved to be an illusion as a practical matter. Empirically, when you make yourself less free, you are not safer, you are just less free.

Part of the weirdness of the reaction this time to the real and horrific threat of terrorism was not the justifiable panic attack after 9/11 ("Quick, let's give the president complete authority to do whatever he thinks is necessary") but the fact that so much of the fear has been orchestrated. Now, you are reading someone who does not believe in conspiracy theories. It would be pleasant to attribute all our difficulties to one great villain, one source of all evil—call it Satan or liberals or fascists or right-wing nutcases or anything else. My experience and reading have convinced me luck, chance, accident, and coincidence are all major players in human history, and if there is one single overriding constant, that would be human stupidity.

Nevertheless, I find it both odd and troubling that so many Straussians are visible in this administration. Leo Strauss was a complex and often opaque European émigré professor at the University of Chicago, often identified as "the father of neoconservatism." Among his followers were Paul Wolfowitz, Ahmad Chalabi, and Zalmay Khalilzad (yep, they went to the University of Chicago). At the end of Gerald Ford's presidency, a group of them, including Wolfowitz, came together in something called Team B. The B-Teamers then believed the CIA, with its many suspect graduates of Ivy League universities, had underestimated the military might of the Soviet Union. If you follow these issues at all, you know that Team B, the neocon guys, who were put in place by then–CIA chief Poppy Bush to second-guess the CIA, were dead wrong. The wheels were coming off the Soviet Union at that point, without us having to do anything. But they scared Jimmy Carter into spending more than was needed on defense. And Team B's delusional reports really worked for Reagan, who added $2 trillion to our national debt in useless military spending, utterly unnecessary at that point. This is not some controversial contention—it's what everyone agrees actually happened. Except maybe some Republican spinmeisters. Reagan's spending spree may have accelerated the process, but the Soviet Union was already rotting from within. So why were the Team B people ever asked back?

The followers of Leo Strauss have a detestable habit of referring dismissively to both the Declaration of Independence and the Constitution of the United States as "the parchment regime." As nearly as I can tell from reading Strauss's work, he rejects all the Enlightenment ideals on which this country was founded and then adds a soupçon of the Nietzschean superman myth. Damned if I know exactly where that puts his followers, but it appears to be somewhere between hypocrisy and cynicism. Whatever they are, I'm damn sure they're not democrats.

Perhaps there is not much more to justice than the plaintive childhood wail "But that's not *fair*!" Grown-ups know life is unfair, but the Constitution of the United States takes a damn good stab at trying to make it equitable under law. There is a school of thought about the Constitution that comes close to secular idolatry, as though the document were a semidivine distillation of all wisdom. I flunk out of that school: except for the first ten or so amendments, the Constitution is amazingly boring reading. But I do think that pretty much everything humankind had learned up to that point, in 1787, about how to prevent injustice, and about how to stop governments from abusing their citizens, is in that document.

I further think the Foundin' Daddies left wiggle room in there, like, here's the basic principles, you can't change them, but adjust or add on the details whenever you need to.

For nearly two terms in office, Team Bush has been undermining what constitutional conservative scholar Bruce Fein calls the "very architecture of the Constitution." And they've had a pretty good run at it.

Let's see, we've already destroyed the Fourth Amendment on unreasonable search and seizure: Has that stopped terrorism cold? Does Osama bin Laden quiver in fear because we have crippled the Fifth and Sixth Amendments?

And the First? Have we defanged Islamist extremists by damaging the First Amendment? Are we any safer? Does this strike you as an effective remedy to terrorism?

Fifth Amendment protections against self-incrimination have been neutered by declaring suspects material witnesses against themselves. Yet neither Brandon Mayfield nor Osama Awadallah provided any information that made any of us any safer. Nor did Abdullah al-Kidd, the University of Idaho football star locked up to testify against someone who had overstayed his visa.

To quote an unlikely source, John Dean, once attorney to

Richard Nixon, "Terrorists can't vanquish their enemies, only hurt them. . . . As horrible as terrorism can be, it must be understood in context. Compared with the policy of mutually assured destruction of the Cold War, with its inherent potential for annihilating humankind, national security experts will tell you privately that terrorism's threat to America appears to fall somewhere between that of killer bees (which scare people but take very few lives) and drunken drivers (who frighten very few people while killing 17,000 annually)."

Permit me, if you will, to address exactly how far back in law we have moved since 9/11. Anybody remember an old potboiler called *The Count of Monte Cristo* by Alexandre Dumas—same guy who wrote *The Three Musketeers*? The plot of this tale of revenge turns on an ancient French legal gizmo called the *lettre de cachet*, literally, a letter of hiding. The story is about a splendid and happy young man who is put away for eighteen years in a dungeon on a fortress prison isle—solely on the strength of anonymous letters of accusation. No trial, no facts, no evidence, no counterargument, just—oops, you've gone down the *oubliette*—the slot into the dungeon. Even by the time of the French Revolution, this clunker of a plot device was antiquated. Not even the *ancien régime* used it much (though it had some notable victims to the end, the Marquis de Sade among them).

Yet, in the United States of America, in 2006, we are now using this very same legal device, centuries gone and utterly discredited. This is not about illegal aliens, or foreign residents, or Arab students—this applies to *citizens of the United States of America*. At any given moment, the president can—without offering any evidence, and without following any rules of procedure—declare any one of us to be a danger, "an enemy combatant," a description for which no legal definition exits.

As we write, Jose Padilla is approaching his fifth year in

prison. For his first twenty-one months, he was not informed of the charges against him. The feds who had him in custody elected to ignore the habeas corpus guarantees that were in place in this country when we were British subjects. By passing President Bush's Military Commissions Act in 2006 (before the November elections), Congress codified that very practice, tossing a thousand years of Anglo-Saxon criminal jurisprudence into the trash.

Since damn few of us were in Afghanistan helping either Osama bin Laden or the Taliban, this may not strike you as a matter of immediate personal interest. But keep in mind, anyone who mentions lost liberties is considered, by George W. Bush's first attorney general, to be guilty of helping terrorists. And as the law is written, by the president's signature, anyone can be deprived of habeas corpus protections. There have been, under this administration, citizens of the United States of America being held in prison without access to a lawyer, without the right to confront their accusers, without the right to a trial, without even knowing the charges against them.

None of the rest of us have any idea if these people are guilty, or even what they are accused of, much less what evidence there might be against them. The whole process is closed, secret, not open to public view. This is a return to the infamous secret proceedings of the Star Chamber court, abolished in England in 1641. Freedom in this country has literally been shoved backward by centuries. Law professors will tell you nothing like this has been known in the West since before King John was forced to sign the Magna Carta in 1215.

Could our government possibly have taken such extreme measures against these few citizens without overwhelming evidence?

Who the hell knows?

The record does not leave a lot of room for optimism.

The late American novelist and essayist John Gardner wrote

that every book needs a guiding metaphor. Here's ours, a John Henry Faulk story I've told so many times that I probably own it by rule of adverse possession.

Years before his career in radio, John Henry was in law enforcement—a Texas Ranger, a captain in fact. He was seven at the time. His friend Boots Cooper, who was six, was sheriff, and the two of them used to do a lot of heavy law enforcement out behind the Faulk place in south Austin. One day Johnny's mama asked them to go down to the henhouse and rout out the chicken snake that had been doing some damage there.

Johnny and Boots loped down to the henhouse on their trusty brooms and commenced to search for the snake. They went all through the nests on the bottom shelf of the henhouse and couldn't find it, so the both of them stood on tippy-toes to look on the top shelf. I myself have never been nose to nose with a chicken snake, but I always took Johnny's word for it that it will just scare the living shit out of you. Scared those boys so bad that they both tried to exit the henhouse at the same time, doing considerable damage to both themselves and the door.

Johnny's mama was a kindly lady, but watching all this, it struck her funny. She was still laughin' when the captain and the sheriff trailed back up to the front porch. "Boys, boys," said Miz Faulk, "what is wrong with you? You know perfectly well a chicken snake cannot hurt you."

That's when Boots Cooper made his semi-immortal observation. "Yes, ma'am," he said, "but there's some things'll scare you so bad, you hurt yourself."

We've allowed ourselves to be scared so bad that we have hurt ourselves. The damage Bush, Cheney, Ashcroft, Gonzales, et al. have done to our Bill of Rights will not be undone unless we act to undo it. The 2006 midterm elections slowed their programmatic assault on the Bill of Rights.

It's now left to all of us who care about this republic to stop it.

BILL OF WRONGS

ONE

Independence Day

Congress shall make no law respecting an establishment of religion, or prohibiting the free exercise thereof; or abridging the freedom of speech, or of the press; or the right of the people peaceably to assemble, and to petition the Government for a redress of grievances.

—First Amendment to the United States Constitution

People should watch what they say.

—White House spokesman Ari Fleischer, October 2001

We were wearing T-shirts, exercising our free-speech rights in the public square. And we were arrested? If you cede this, there's nothing left.

—University of Houston law student Jeff Rank, February 2007

It's July 4, 2004.

The temperature is in the mid-nineties, the humidity is high, the crowd on the West Virginia capitol grounds numbers three, or four, or six thousand, depending on the media source. George W. Bush is in a tight race with John Kerry. And a growing number of voters have already gone south on Bush's war in Iraq.

After Representative Shelley Moore Capito introduces the president, he thanks her for serving as his state campaign chair. Then takes ten more minutes to make it through the acknowledgments and howdies in his twenty-five-minute speech. He thanks the Boy Scouts. And the Girl Scouts. He thanks Charleston's Republican mayor, Danny Jones. He thanks country and western singer Aaron Tippin. He thanks the minister of Bible Center megachurch, whose service he missed that morning because of a mechanical problem on Air Force One. He thanks no one in particular for the "coal found in West Virginia." He thanks the Almighty a few times. He even thanks the West Virginia Coal Association president, whom he describes as "my friend," for getting the coal out of the ground and into the nation's power plants. He doesn't thank the coal miners, but the president is doubled over with gratitude.

The party dignitaries, Bush's state campaign chair, the planned stop at a big-box evangelical church, the Bush T-shirts worn by enthusiastic supporters, all suggest that the Fourth of July visit to Charleston is a campaign event.

It's not. It's an official visit of the president of the United States, with taxpayers picking up the tab for *Air Force One*, the president's security detail, and the weeks of work by the White House Advance Team. But political strategist Karl Rove is in charge, the Iraq war in question, and John Kerry slightly ahead in national polls. So the president delivers his well-rehearsed keep-fear-alive campaign stem-winder, written to drive home the message he hopes will close the deal in November: *The terrorists who were plotting to attack us again are hard on the run in Afghanistan and Iraq*.

> Our immediate task in battlefronts like Iraq and Afghanistan and elsewhere is to capture or kill the terrorists. That's our immediate task. We made a decision. You see. We will engage these

> enemies in these countries around the world so we do not have to face them at home. (*Applause*) After the attacks of September the eleventh, 2001, the nation resolved to fight terrorists where they dwell. (*Applause*) You can't talk sense to them. You can't negotiate with them. You cannot hope for the best with these people. We must be relentless and determined to do our duty. (*Applause*)

But it's the Fourth of July, and just as a good country and western song requires the mention of Mama, trains, trucks, prison, and gettin' drunk, there are certain de rigueur requirements of a good Fourth of July speech. Bush touched on most of them: the Founders, George Washington ("I call him George W."), God, the Troops, abstractions like Democracy and Freedom.

> On this Fourth of July, we confirm our love of freedom, the freedom for people to speak their minds, the freedom of people to worship as they so choose. (*Applause*) Free thought, free expression, that's what we believe. But we also understand that that freedom is not America's gift to the world. Freedom is the Almighty God's gift to each man and woman in this world. (*Applause*) And by serving that ideal, by never forgetting the values and the principles that have made this country so strong 228 years after our country's founding, we will bring hope to others and at the same time make America more secure. (*Applause*)

Nicole Rank had moved from Bush's home state to Charleston, West Virginia, to work on a FEMA flood control project. When agency employees were offered tickets to the president's Fourth of July event, she filled out an online application for herself and her husband, Jeff, who had followed her from their home in Corpus Christi. Neither of them was a George W. Bush supporter. But that question didn't appear on the form the Secret Service required of anyone attending the official presidential visit.

Both, in fact, were opponents of the war in Iraq. Both received tickets to the event.

The Ranks showed up for the president's visit to the capitol, made their way through the security checkpoint and to a place near where Bush was to speak. Then they took off their shirts to uncover homemade T-shirts with the international ⃠ symbol over the word "Bush."

A bold gesture in a rabidly pro-Bush crowd.

Team Bush believes it only takes a few antiwar protesters to muck up a pro-war speech. A sixteen-year-old volunteer spotted the Ranks and ran to warn Tom Hamm that two people were creating a problem. Thomas Donald Hamm was an unemployed thirty-year-old event volunteer who had worked on Shelley Moore Capito's campaign and in her congressional office. He's young, but he's decisive. He surveyed the situation and summarily suspended the First Amendment, telling the couple the T-shirts had to go or they had to leave.

When Jeff Rank told Hamm he was breaking no law and refused to take off his shirt, Hamm called for backup: Aaron Spork, who actually was working in Capito's D.C. office. Together they made it clear: no First Amendment protections on the Fourth of July in Charleston, West Virginia. Hamm called a capitol police officer and told him the Ranks' tickets were revoked.

At which point, the revoking got under way.

Nicole Rank was nimble enough to whip out her disposable camera and photograph everyone who confronted her. Then the Ranks sat on the ground, to indicate they were not leaving. At approximately 11:00 A.M. they were handcuffed and led from the capitol grounds by the capitol police officer who first responded and a state trooper and protective services officer who showed up as an "arrest team." Reporters who tried to speak to them were waved off by Hamm, who told them if they followed the couple out, they would not be allowed back in and would miss the president's speech.

As Jeff Rank recalled, the band on the platform played "America the Beautiful" as the Ranks were frog-marched to the police van that would take them to the Charleston municipal jail.

President Bush started speaking at exactly 12:57. By the time he got to the constitutional rights properly enshrined in the First Amendment—"our love of freedom, the freedom for people to speak their minds. . . . Free thought, free expression, that's what we believe"—Jeff and Nicole Rank already had their handcuffs removed and were sitting in separate cells in Charleston's police department building. "It was chickenshit," said Nitro, West Virginia, lawyer Harvey Peyton. "I mean these young kids, these twenty-somethings, just told the officers, 'Their tickets are revoked, get them off the capitol grounds.' "

It was one of several varieties of chickenshit expressly prohibited by the First Amendment, even if it took the Congress and the courts a while to make that prohibition clear. Law professor Geoffrey Stone begins his book *Perilous Times: Free Speech in Wartime* with a description of the first fight over the First Amendment. It occurred less than ten years after the Bill of Rights was ratified, during what Stone refers to as the "half war" with France, which almost happened in the 1790s after the American government stiffed the French. France had stepped in and salvaged the American Revolution. When the U.S. government refused to support the French in their war against Britain, the government in Paris declared all U.S. sailors pirates and began boarding U.S. ships.

President John Adams responded by putting the nation on war footing, adding eighteen new divisions to the Army, and calling George Washington back from Mount Vernon to take command. Adams's Federalist majority in Congress singled out immigrants, suspending jury trials and allowing indefinite detention of foreigners when the nation was at war. Then they turned their attention to American citizens, passing a sedition act that provided for a two-year sentence and $2,000 fine for anyone who would "write, print, utter, or publish" scandalous, untrue, or malicious comments against either house of Congress or the president.

Vermont congressman Matthew Lyon was the first person tried under the Sedition Act. He said that under President Adams "every consideration of the public law [was] swallowed up in a continual grasp for power, in an unbounded thirst for ridiculous pomp, foolish adulation, and selfish avarice."

Lyon got no jail time for that when he said it. But he made the mistake of quoting himself after Adams signed the Sedition Act into law. He was prosecuted by Secretary of State Timothy Pickering, fined $1,000 plus $60.96 in court costs, and jailed four months in conditions we today associate with Donald Rumsfeld's extraordinary rendition. Lyon described a damp, freezing cell, which included a "necessary" with the stench "equal to the Philadelphia docks in the month of August."

Since Matthew Lyon was locked up in 1798, the notion that a citizen can be arrested for offending the president has given way to free-speech protections that are almost as sacrosanct as high school football in Texas. James Madison declared the Sedition Act unconstitutional because it returned American citizens to the status of subjects—reinstating the "exploded doctrine that 'the administrators of the Government are the masters, and not the servants, of the people.' "

Law professor Leonard Levy—who seems to do little else but think and write about the Constitution—writes that seditious speech is an alien concept to American democracy. It only exists "where people are subjects rather than sovereigns and their criticism implies contempt of their master."

It's a bold, simple concept, spelled out in the First Amendment and shaped by two centuries of criminal and civil jurisprudence: George III was a master. George W. is a servant. On the 228th birthday of the United States, that principle got turned on its head in Charleston. In a scene that might have been lifted from a *Mayberry R.F.D.* script, an arrest team of officers from three jurisdictions—the city, capitol, and state—stood in earshot of the couple sitting in the jail cells, arguing over who was expected to charge them. And with what offense. It was the Charleston city jail, so the city of Charleston settled on criminal trespass. The real charge was the same one Matthew Lyon got popped for in 1798: seditious speech. The couple locked up in the Charleston jail were there because they insulted the president.

The Ranks were issued citations and released on their own recognizance—with instructions to go nowhere near the capitol grounds, where President Bush was speaking. It was a little late. By the time they got back to the hotel, the local TV news was already running a clip of the president's speech—the passage where he described "free thought, free expression." Nicole and Jeff Rank had been dragged from the capitol grounds in handcuffs, jailed, booked, released, and, as they walked from the jail to their hotel, recognized by people on the streets who had seen them on the TV news. "We were sitting in a hotel room rubbing our wrists and he's talking about freedom of expression," said Jeff Rank. "Is he kidding?"

It would get worse.

Monday, July 5, was a holiday for federal workers. On Tuesday morning, Nicole Rank was summoned from a 9:30 meeting by her supervisor's administrative assistant. FEMA's federal coordinating officer and his legal counsel were waiting for her. "They told me that, because of my actions, I had compromised FEMA's mission in West Virginia," she said. They reassured her that she wasn't fired, then ordered her to clean out her desk, turn in her rental car, and check out of the hotel where she was living on a FEMA per diem account. She would be responsible for any hotel expense incurred after July 6.

It felt like fired.

That night the Ranks left West Virginia and drove to Philadelphia, where Nicole had worked in FEMA's offices before being assigned to disaster relief in West Virginia. They spent a couple of days in a Motel 6, cleaning out their storage unit and loading what would fit in their Jeep station wagon—along with their dog and cat. Then they started the three-day drive back home to Texas. Before they drove too far south, they stopped in Virginia to phone the court clerk in Charleston. Their citation specified that fines could be mailed in if the infraction did not involve domestic violence or DUI. The clerk told Jeff Rank they would have to make a court appearance in two weeks: "She said, 'I don't care what the ticket says, you have to come in.' "

On the drive from Roanoke, Virginia, to Charleston, West Virginia, Jeff and Nicole Rank decided they had been pushed too far. "We were wearing T-shirts," Jeff said in an interview in the couple's Houston apartment. "Exercising our freedom of speech in a public square. . . . And they were treating us like criminals."

"Our costs were mounting, we had to stay in Charleston until the fifteenth, so I picked up the phone and called the ACLU," said Nicole. ACLU staff attorney Terri Baur began to explain that there was a two- to three-week process that began with submitting a written request for ACLU representation. Then something clicked. "She said, 'Are you Nicole Rank? We've been looking everywhere for you.' "

Baur said that the West Virginia board members were at a meeting in San Francisco and upon their return would almost certainly vote to represent the Ranks. She even found the couple a cabin to stay in while they awaited trial. Out of work, money, and luck, Nicole Rank had made the right phone call.

Harvey Peyton was eager to take the case. The feds had trashed the Ranks' First Amendment rights and done it in a cowardly way, using local law enforcement as the heavies. "One of them is a capitol policeman," Peyton said. "One of them is a conservation officer. Two are Charleston policemen. And one is a West Virginia state trooper. They had no instruction, no training, no training about how to handle a protest. . . . So they give them to the Charleston Police Department, who don't know what to do with them because they didn't break the law."

Peyton looked at the municipal code and concluded that the trespassing charge wouldn't stick. "This wasn't going to be the most difficult case I'd ever tried. It was like trespassing in the public library," he said.

The Ranks' trial was scheduled for 7:00 A.M. on July 15 in municipal court.

"I walked in the city courthouse that day," Peyton said. "They got a real smart mayor in Charleston, West Virginia. His name is Danny Jones. Now, he's a Republican, but he's not a Bush Republican. His knuckles don't drag the ground. And I'm thinking, Well, the mayor's here. It's seven o'clock in the morning. It's municipal court. And the mayor's here?"

So was the press. To get into a courthouse filled with DUI defendants, Jeff and Nicole Rank had to do a perp walk through a gauntlet of TV cameras and radio and newspaper reporters. "I felt like O.J.," Jeff said. "And all we had done was exercise our First Amendment right of free speech."

As soon as Peyton entered the courtroom, the assistant city attorney walked over and said the city would move to drop the charges. "The mayor told them to dismiss it," Peyton said. "Then he went next Monday to the city council and had the council pass a motion apologizing to the Ranks. It took the sting out of it."

But not enough.

Jeff Rank is short and stocky. His close-cropped brown beard and gold metal-frame glasses tend to focus an intensity that becomes more evident when he leans forward to listen or talk. Nicole is quieter and more pensive, her longer Byzantine icon face framed by dark hair. "She's wicked smart," says Jeff, as he describes his wife passing the written exam and making it through the round of interviews that qualified her for a position as a Foreign Service officer—only to be told that she failed her security clearance because she had been arrested in Charleston. (He admits he failed the written test, which they took together.)

Two and a half years after their arrest on "seditious speech" charges, they moved on. To a small apartment ten miles from downtown Houston, crammed full of bookshelves and fish tanks. Nicole's employer, FEMA, had brought her back on in Charleston. But both she and Jeff had other plans. Nicole enrolled in a master's program in social work at the University of Houston; Jeff enrolled in the University of Houston law school; Abbie, their seven-month-old daughter, enrolled in the university day-care program.

They are saving frequent flyer miles to return to Charleston, where they have filed suit against Gregory Jenkins, the deputy director of the White House Office of Presidential Advance; Secret Service director W. Ralph Basham; and John Does 1 through 4, who have since been identified because Nicole photographed everyone involved in their arrest.

From his New York office, ACLU senior attorney Chris Hansen describes what seems like a perfect fact situation: "It was an official presidential visit. It was open to the public. Our clients got their tickets in the way they were supposed to get their tickets. It's very clear that they were excluded because of the content of the message on their T-shirts."

Hansen intends to "establish responsibility." The federal government plays a shell game and is, he says, "coy about admitting that it excludes people who disagree with them, particularly from official presidential visits."

Conforming to the cowardly behavior Harvey Peyton describes, the feds claimed qualified immunity and asked the judge to dismiss the charges against them. To continue the pretrial process of discovery and keep the case alive, the Ranks had to add local police officers as defendants. "They [the federal officials] were telling them to get these people out of here," said Peyton. "And the officers had no bones about it. They were told the tickets had been revoked and the Ranks had to leave." He describes the local cops as "victims" of federal officials who refuse to stand up and defend their policy.

Jeff Rank will be out of law school before the case is decided and Nicole perhaps enrolled in one of the "dream law schools" she's applied to. Neither of the two seems inclined to back away from the lawsuit styled *Jeffrey Rank and Nicole Rank v. Gregory J. Jenkins, Deputy Assistant to the President of the United States and Director of the White House Office of Presidential Advance, et al.*

We aren't required to earn the rights defined in the first ten amendments of America's Constitution. Like God's grace, they are unconditionally conferred on all of us. W. Bush, in fact, believes they are God's grace. He often says so. He did while Nicole and Jeff Rank were being mugged and fingerprinted in the Charleston jail and he was telling an Independence Day crowd at the West Virginia capitol that the brand of democracy we enjoy in the United States is God's gift to every man and woman in every country. Even if we have to give Divine Providence a little goose once in a while—in places like Iraq.

If free-speech rights were something we had to earn, Sue Niederer comes as close as any of us to earning them. Her twenty-four-year-old son, Seth Dvorin, was a brand-new first lieutenant in the Army, home on leave from Iraq in January 2004. While Seth and his new bride, Kelly, were staying with her, Niederer overheard her son arguing with his commander at Fort Drum. Her soft-spoken boy was shouting into the phone in a voice she had never heard, increasing in volume, repeating the same phrases:

"I *need* GPS security systems. I *need* computers. My men need these or they're going to be dead!"

Less than a month later, her son was dead. Killed by an improvised explosive device near Iskanderiya—a Sunni town south of Baghdad that British journalist Robert Fisk describes as "throat-cutting country where insurgents man their own checkpoints beside the palm groves and canals."

On a cold Sunday morning three years after her son died in Iraq, Sue Niederer sits in a small office in a large house in New Jersey. She's a short, stout woman, with close-cropped, styled gray hair, a natural scowl, and a working-class Jersey congeniality. She says Seth enlisted after he graduated from Rutgers and was sent "on a suicide mission." After he was told by recruiters that his rank and specialty would keep him out of combat, her son was ordered to Iraq the day he arrived at Fort Drum. His commanding officer told him "they need officers in Iraq," she says.

"They say he was a hero. But they literally sent my son on a suicide mission," says Niederer. "He was murdered by this administration."

Sue Niederer seems beyond tears.

She opposed the war and regretted her son's decision to enlist. After he was killed, she converted her grief into her own small antiwar campaign, speaking and marching at protests, picketing and pamphleting outside the White House, camping and protesting near the entrance to the president's ranch in Texas.

She's vigilant. When someone from the Bush administration shows up anywhere near Trenton, New Brunswick, or Princeton, Sue Niederer is waiting to greet him. Colin Powell can confirm that.

So Niederer was surprised to get on the list for Laura Bush's mid-September 2004 campaign visit to Hamilton. She wanted to attend but knew that access to the event was controlled by the local Republican Party. She was a high-decibel critic of Bush's war in Iraq. She had just spoken at a protest in front of Republican congressman Chris Smith's district office in Hamilton. And members of Smith's staff were at the Republican Party office, inputting the information the Secret Service required of anyone attending the first lady's event.

It was a tough ticket.

There was a separate and perfectly valid reason to deny Sue Niederer admission to Laura Bush's New Jersey speech, which had nothing to do with the Bushies' peculiar interpretation of the First Amendment. Three months after her son died in Iraq, a reporter from *CounterPunch* had asked Niederer if she was aware of the growing body of evidence that the war was waged on misinformation. She was. In a response she says was motivated by anger and grief, Sue Niederer tore into George W. Bush: "I wanted to rip the president's head off. Curse him, yell at him, call him a self-righteous bastard, shoot him in the groined area. Let him suffer."

Not the sort of thing one says to a reporter.

Yet a woman from Congressman Smith's district office said "Hi, Sue," as one of the Mercer County Republicans volunteers handed Niederer a ticket to see the First Lady in Hamilton—a township fifteen minutes from Niederer's Pennington, New Jersey, home. And nine miles downriver from the stretch of the Delaware George Washington crossed on Christmas Day 1776.

Once inside the Colonial Fire Hall in Hamilton, Niederer put on the desert fatigue hat Seth had given her when he left for Iraq months earlier and removed a long-sleeved shirt to reveal a T-shirt bearing a photographic image of her son under bold block lettering that read:

PRESIDENT BUSH: YOU KILLED MY SON.

No one paid much attention, though a man standing nearby said his son had served in Seth's unit in Iraq. When Laura Bush began speaking about the war, Niederer stood up and shouted: "Why aren't your children serving?" She was swarmed by young volunteers carrying placards, who had instructions to surround any protester, hold up their signs, and chant: "Four more years! Four more years!"

The commotion caught the attention of the first lady's security detail.

Laura Bush might have seized that moment. Confronted by a grieving mother who had lost her son a few months earlier, she might have paused and asked Sue Niederer to meet with her in private after the event concluded. A mother—"a mom," as George W. says—of twin daughters two years younger than Seth Dvorin was when his life ended in Iraq might empathize.

For a moment Niederer thought that might happen. She had overestimated the compassion and agility of the first lady. "Her jaw dropped and her face froze when I spoke," Niederer said.

"Then I saw the Secret Service agents," she went on. "They came over and said, 'We want you out of here, you're trespassing.' " Niederer held up her ticket to the event and said she wanted to speak to the reporters who had gathered around her.

Agents pushed her to the exit and turned her over to local police. "They threw her in the paddy wagon like a piece of luggage," said her husband, Greg, who sat quietly for most of the interview. Niederer was handcuffed and driven to a parking lot at the police station, where she was held for what she believes was forty-five minutes. She was then led into the jail and handcuffed to a wall, while the local police puzzled over charges that would fit the crime.

"I asked them, 'What are you charging me with?' " she said. "They said, 'Truthfully, we don't know, but right now we're charging you with defiant trespassing and disrupting a public event.' "

At the firehouse, Secret Service agents had pushed Niederer past reporters and into a police van. After she was arraigned and returned to her cell to be released, the Hamilton police offered her a better deal. She could quietly depart through the back door of the station. Or, the officer on the jail desk told her, she could walk out through the front door—"where all the media is."

"You want to go out the front door, don't you?" he asked.

With a wink and a nod, a New Jersey cop restored the free-speech rights the U.S. Secret Service had denied Sue Niederer. She held an impromptu press conference. But Elvis had left the building. Laura Bush had concluded her remarks and was off to the airport.

Sue Niederer was ordered to appear in court one month after her arrest. Two weeks later she learned by reading *The Times* of Trenton that all charges against her were dropped. (In municipal court documents, we found that they were dropped the day after her arrest.)

After Niederer publicly offended the first lady, the FBI got around to investigating the comments she had made about the president months earlier. Niederer learned about that investigation by reading *The Times* of Trenton, though she suspected something was up because cars she'd never before seen were regularly parking in her cul-de-sac. Nothing came of the investigation. Either "shoot him in the groined area" didn't rise to the level of a threat against the president, or the prosecution of a grieving mother was too unseemly.

Niederer wanted to file suit. The New Jersey ACLU offered to represent her. But she feared a lawsuit would either end her marriage or damage her husband's relationship with his family.

In January, three years after her son spent his last few nights in his family home, Sue Niederer was preparing for a peace march in Washington at the end of the month.

"I protest," she said. "It's what I do."

In February 2004, the quiet of the Alpine valley that provided the setting for Thomas Mann's *The Magic Mountain* was shattered by the growl of a squadron of Apache and Blackhawk attack helicopters escorting one larger Sikorsky assault helicopter. As the Sikorsky landed and the other aircraft circled overhead, vans with dark tinted windows appeared, and armed agents bearing American flag lapel pins and telltale earpieces poured out of the vehicles, some leading dogs on leashes. What residents of the tranquil Swiss town might have believed was an armed military assault was instead the arrival of Vice President Dick Cheney and his foreign-travel security detachment.

Former U.S. president Bill Clinton; U.N. secretary-general Kofi Annan; French foreign minister Dominique de Villepin; U.S. commerce secretary Don Evans; and even Pakistani president Pervez Musharraf, who had already survived two assassination attempts, had all arrived with little public notice.

Cheney's arrival was different.

"It was an embarrassment," said a State Department official who witnessed Cheney landing. "It shattered the quiet of a little valley. His obsession with security is real. National security and personal security, too. He was the only head of state [*sic*] who needed Blackhawk helicopters to escort him to the G8 meeting. It was Switzerland, for God's sake."

In the summer of 2006, Steve Howards walked into Dick Cheney's security obsession. Howards is a Denver environmental consultant. In June 2006 his two sons were attending a piano camp in Beaver Creek Village, a ski lodge and mountain resort 120 miles west of Denver. Like 66 percent of Americans at that particular moment, Steve Howards opposed the war in Iraq. And standing in Beaver Creek Village plaza on June 7 was the man most responsible for planning, starting, and prosecuting the war. Flanked by about twenty Secret Service agents, Dick Cheney was working a small crowd. Howards walked up to the vice president and said: "I think your policies in Iraq are reprehensible." Then Howards and his ten-year-old son walked away. "All of this happened in less than fifty seconds," Howards said.

Ten minutes later, as Howards and his younger son were walking back to the condo where they were staying, Secret Service agent Virgil "Gus" Reichle stepped in front of him and asked if he had assaulted the vice president. When Howards said no, the agent asked him if he had touched the vice president.

Howards recounted, “He said, ‘If you touched the vice president, that’s tantamount to assaulting the vice president.’

“I said, ‘I told Mr. Cheney how I feel about his Iraq policy. If he doesn’t want to hear public criticism, you should help him avoid contact with the public.’ ”

As Reichle questioned him, Howards heard agents who had gathered around asking each other if anyone had witnessed him touching the vice president. Then Reichle dispatched an agent into the crowd to look for someone who might have seen Steve Howards touch the vice president. The agent returned with a man who said he had.

“After he tried to find an agent who would back up what he thought happened, he had to go into the crowd to find a witness,” Howards said. “I mean, it was immediately evident that this was nothing but harassment and a very contrived effort to fabricate a case of assault.”

Agent Reichle informed Howards that he was going to be charged with assaulting the vice president and placed under arrest.

As Howards was being searched and handcuffed, his son panicked and ran to his mother in the condo. “I felt like I was in Tiananmen Square,” Howards said. “It was so ironic. I was in a mall in a ski resort and I was being handcuffed and taken away for speaking to the vice president.”

Howards was turned over to local deputies and driven to the Eagle County jail, which had once housed celebrity defendant Kobe Bryant. While he was in custody, Reichle told Howards he was talking to the DA to make sure that assault charges were filed. Howards was charged with harassment, though Reichle pulled Howards’s wife aside in the waiting area to tell her he intended to get the charges bumped up to assault.

Six weeks later, a Secret Service agent showed up at Howards’s Denver office while he was out, flashed his badge to a lawyer who worked there, but refused to leave a name or phone number. "It's Gestapo-ish," Howards said. "It's harassment. When people come to your place of work, refusing to even leave their name so you can call them back."

Howards and his wife, Deborah, worried that the government would increase the charges. In late September, the Eagle County DA informed Steve Howards that all charges against him were dismissed.

"That's what really ticked me off. When they dropped the charge," Howards said. "It was their acknowledgment of how transparently abusive this was.

"I was relieved, but I was furious. They had handcuffed me in front of my kids in a public place. And they made an extraordinary effort to attack and disparage me in the media. To disparage me as a crazy on TV news in Metro Denver 8."

Howards considered filing suit but wondered about reprisals. He's a consultant and has government contracts. "I began asking my friends," he said. "Half of them said yes, because it's the right thing to do. Half said don't do it, because of the retribution it might bring." He filed suit, he said, not in response to the friends who encouraged him but in reaction to those who said not to do it.

"They are—we are—scared of their own government. We are scared of tax audits, of loss of contracts," Howards said. "We are, we as a people, have acquiesced on our constitutional rights because we have a very real fear of retribution if we challenge the government. What I see is this incremental sacrifice of our constitutional rights because we fear our own government."

Howards retained Denver lawyer David Lane and filed suit in federal court. The complaint Lane drafted describes the violation of his client's First and Fourth Amendment rights.

Reichle filed a response that says Howards was belligerent and said "fuck you" when he was stopped. The attorneys representing the agent also suggested that Howards might have been carrying a needle with which he could have injected some poison into the vice president's arm when he touched him—a claim Lane dismisses as absurd: "Everybody out there was backslapping and shaking Cheney's hand. He happened to be the only person who was critical of Cheney."

The suit asks for damages, but Lane is after something larger than a monetary award. He is looking for the chain of command. Who ordered the suppression of his client's free-speech rights? Is there, within the Secret Service, a custom, practice, and policy of suppressing these rights?

Howards says it's hard to know how many people have been arrested for publicly disagreeing with the president. The stories that make the news usually involve someone filing suit. Most people hunker down and hope the charges will be dropped or pay their fines and do their time.

Some brave citizens fight back. And they change policy

None of the lawsuits filed against the president's Secret Service and Advance Office has yet made it to trial. But Greg Jenkins on the White House Advance Team is less inclined to push local authorities to be so thuggish during presidential visits. Gus Reichle won't be so trigger-happy next time a citizen says something that annoys Dick Cheney. And when Secret Service agents leaned on him a second time, Charleston mayor Danny Jones, whose heart and head were never in the prosecution of Jeff and Nicole Rank, told them to shove it. President Bush would have to live with antiwar protesters lined up on the South Side Bridge on July 27, 2006—or he could find another route to Shelley Moore Capito's fundraiser.

Three years after an arrest team dragged Jeff and Nicole Rank away from their president's July 4 speech, the federal government settled. In August 2007 the government paid the Ranks $80,000 in damages, while admitting no wrongdoing. They didn't have to. A "Presidential Advance Manual," published by the Office of Presidential Advance, confirmed what the Ranks, Steven Howards, and Sue Niederer learned when they tried to exercise their free speech rights in the presence of the president or vice president. It was all spelled out in the manual—or at least, in what wasn't redacted. All but twenty of the one-hundred-twelve pages of the manual were completely blank. Yet in the scant information available is evidence of a White House program to suppress political speech that might embarrass the president—even when that speech is protected by the First Amendment.

Most damning are recommendations regarding the use of "rally squads" to surround potential protestors with signs or large banners to obscure them from the view of the press. "These squads should be instructed to always look for demonstrators. The rally squad's task is to use their signs and banners as shields between the demonstrators and the main press platform. If the demonstrators are yelling out, rally squads can begin and lead supportive chants to drown out protestors (USA! USA! USA!). As a last resort, security should remove the demonstrators from the event site. The rally squads can include, but are not limited to, college/young republican [*sic*] organizations, local athletic teams, and fraternities/sororities. . . . At least one squad should be 'roaming' throughout the perimeter of the event to look for potential problems."

Volunteers were urged to contact the Secret Service if they encountered anyone who represented an actual threat to the president, but to use their own resources to deal with someone who might embarrass the president or attract the media's attention.

Volunteers and advance team members were told to "decide if the solution would cause more negative publicity than if the demonstrators were simply left alone."

They clearly miscalculated with Jeff and Nicole Rank.

Steven Howards describes taking the government to court as something akin to civic duty. "If more people would respond this way, and maybe I'm naïve, the Secret Service and the government would think longer about whether or not to harass people in an attempt to discourage them from exercising rights that are guaranteed by the Constitution."

TWO

A Zone of Their Own

I'm all in favor of a free-speech zone. I think it should be the United States of America. This notion that there should be places where you can engage in free speech and places where you can't is totally antithetical to the Constitution.

—Congressman Barney Frank, May 2003

Rifle in hand, pistol tucked in his belt (legal 'cause "we're Texas"), and holding a sign that reads HERE TO SHOOT THE PRESIDENT (admittedly problematic), a reporter set out to road test his theory that the designated "free-speech zone" in Crawford, Texas, was so remote it was invisible. Ten miles from G. W. Bush's Prairie Chapel Ranch, the reporter would stand like a desert stylite in silent protest for one hour. After no one noticed, he would return to his office to bang out 1,000 words about the absurdity of a "free-speech zone" so isolated that any free speechifying was inaudible.

Despite reassurances that neither gun would be loaded, and an offer to use toy weapons, his editor considered the reporter's idea irresponsible, if inspired. So "The Best Little Free-Speech Zone in Texas" was never reported, written, or published.

Odds are he would have pulled it off.

Not because such an offensive act would have been tolerated by the citizens of Crawford. Crawford adores its favorite favorite son, even if he didn't adopt the hard-bitten Central Texas town until the second year of his second term as governor. The love is understandable. He was our governor. He's our president. We're a patriotic state. And, until George and Laura bought the ranch, in 1999, commerce was a town in Hunt County, almost two hundred miles from Crawford. Only after the Western White House was up and going did some pulse of retail commerce return to Crawford's moribund Main Street.

Maybe it's because nobody ever opened a souvenir shop to sell Bill of Rights T-shirts, but for whatever reason, the citizens of Crawford (pop. 789) and their elected officials are not so devoted to the First Amendment. Critical comments are redacted from guest books in gift shops selling GWB memorabilia. High school students are warned about clothing that implies disrespect for the president. And protest, if it has to happen, is confined to the "free-speech zone" situated between the Crawford Pirates football stadium and the school district bus barn.

Texas towns have a tradition of turning their dislikes into city ordinances: no liquor in Lubbock; no dancin' in Anson; no blacks in the white sections of public housing in Vidor. But the extent to which Crawford would go to shield the president from all dissent was extreme even by the standards of the Great State. Two years after Bush took office, Crawford's protective bubble for the president was challenged, putting the Constitution to a test before a Texas jury that was a sure bet to pick order over law.

The trouble started, as it often does in Texas, with a foreigner.

On May 3, 2003, Australian prime minister John Howard became "the first foreign leader to actually visit the people of Crawford in the business district," according to the town website. Howard bought a "Friends and Allies" coffee mug at the Western White House Gift Shop, for Tony Blair's fiftieth birthday. While the prime minister of Australia was buying the prime minister of England a cheap gift that would only remind him of his canine fidelity to the president of the United States, an antiwar protest was under way in Austin. As the rally broke up, a small group decided to drive north and continue the protest near the entrance to the president's sixteen-hundred-acre ranch. Austin middle school teacher Ken Zafiris said they hoped to take advantage of the press pack following the Australian prime minister. "We were going to go out to the gate of Bush's ranch and make our statement and put up our signs, then go home."

To get to the ranch, a dozen cars traveling north from Austin had to drive through Crawford. There they ran into a blockade of ten police cars and fifty state and local law enforcement officers. All under the command of Crawford's chief of police, Donnie Tidmore. As the out-of-towners got out of their cars, the police chief warned that they were in violation of Crawford's parade ordinance and allowed them three minutes to get back into their cars, turn around, and get the hell out of Crawford.

Several members of the group approached the chief's car and reassured him they had no intention of stopping in Crawford and less interest in moving to the "free-speech zone" behind the bus barn. They were in Crawford because the town is situated between Austin and George Bush's Prairie Chapel Ranch. The chief turned on his bullhorn and began a countdown punctuated by dips into a chewing tobacco pack and warnings that anyone not in a car and prepared to leave town when three minutes was up was going to jail. Across the street from the blocked cars, a group of George Bush supporters—mostly boys in their teens and early twenties—waved Texas, American, and Confederate flags and shouted at the protesters. The scene was so Southern Gothic that a day-tripper down from Dallas might have confused it with a movie shoot.

When the police chief gave the order at the end of his three-minute countdown, four people who hadn't returned to their cars were arrested, along with a long-haired man who had walked down the street from the Crawford "Peace House" to check out the blockade. All five were held in a police van for about an hour, then driven to Waco, where they spent eighteen hours in jail. The following day, they were charged with protesting without a permit, told that a date would be set for them to appear in municipal court in Crawford, and released with instructions not to go back to Crawford.

In Austin, they contacted James Harrington, the legal director of the Texas Civil Rights Project. Harrington is a constitutional lawyer who teaches at the University of Texas law school. He's been trying First Amendment cases since he was the ACLU's staff attorney in Austin twenty years earlier. He has a lined, bearded face and wears a perpetual scowl that belies a wry sense of humor. The trial in municipal court in Crawford would be one of his more memorable (and humorous) cases.

"The crowd was so big that they moved it from the municipal courtroom to the city auditorium," Harrington said. "It was packed. When we walked in, you could hear the soft thud of kangaroos bouncing around."

Harrington described the trial as a day of "political theater." The municipal judge recused himself because he had been involved in drafting the antiprotest ordinance Harrington would have to challenge in order to defend his clients. He was replaced by a local sportscaster with a rich baritone and a poor grasp of the law, who also served as justice of the peace. The substitute judge compensated for his lack of experience by consulting the city attorney, who eagerly answered his questions regarding law and procedure.

The case was so controversial that the substitute judge summoned sixty prospective jurors to impanel a jury of six, and a security detail of almost as many Crawford city police officers and county sheriffs. "They were convinced the terrorists were on trial," said Harrington. During voir dire, the process by which lawyers screen and select a jury, several prospective jurors shouted at the defense attorney, complaining that Harrington was wasting the taxpayers' money.

"When I asked how many of them had an opinion that [my protesting clients] shouldn't have been doing this, about half the people in the room raised their hands," said Harrington. "And then, there was this minister sitting in the front row, who was wearing his collar. I asked him, 'Do you think you can be fair?' And he said, 'Well, I really don't think so.' "

At issue was a city ordinance Harrington described as a throwback to the pre-civil-rights era—prohibiting any "procession, parade, or demonstration" without fifteen days' notice and the approval of the police chief. The ordinance had been selectively applied to Harrington's clients. Shortly after the five antiwar protesters were locked in the police van, the local kids, waving Confederate, Texas, and U.S. flags, fell into a bedraggled parade behind a police car driving down one of Crawford's main thoroughfares. None of the flag-waving locals taunting the protesters was arrested.

As the trial unfolded, the chief of police testified that one person walking down a Crawford street while wearing a political button could be "a sign of a demonstration." If such a person did not have a valid permit issued under Crawford's parade ordinance, he would be subject to arrest. Under cross-examination, the chief struggled to define a parade or procession but concluded that fifteen cars and a bus, or twenty cars without a bus, driving together through Crawford without a permit would constitute an illegal parade. He agreed that the Crawford Pirates' homecoming caravan, which came through town every fall without a permit, was subject to arrest—even if he would never actually subject the homecomers to arrest.

The jury found nothing wrong with the facts as explained by Chief Tidmore or the law as explicated by the city attorney. Six jurors quickly found five defendants guilty. Four were fined the five-hundred-dollar maximum allowed by the ordinance. The local peace hippie, who wore an anti-Bush button as he walked down the street to check out the roadblock, was fined three hundred dollars. Perhaps because he was a guilty innocent bystander. Or because the police denied him his medication while he was jailed for eighteen hours, after ignoring his entreaties to use a bathroom while he was locked in the van (causing him to relieve himself in his pants).

Harrington said he would appeal, and the city council promptly repealed the statute. If the handwriting wasn't on the wall (also illegal in Crawford), it was spelled out in more than one case handed down by the U.S. Supreme Court. On point was a civil suit in which the National Park Service was slapped down for denying a permit to antiabortion protesters who wanted to express their opposition to President Bill Clinton during his second inauguration parade down Pennsylvania Avenue: "The government cannot exclude from a public gathering in a public forum on no other basis those citizens whose views it fears or dislikes or prevent their peaceful expression of those views."

The "Crawford Five" case was scheduled for review by a county court at law, the standard appellate venue for municipal courts in Texas. In his appeal, Harrington described an unconstitutional ordinance that had "mutated from a 'mild' example of content-based regulation to an extraordinary vehicle for suppression of political belief and expression unpopular with the Crawford police chief." When Harrington subpoenaed Police Chief Tidmore, the city of

Crawford folded. To avoid another trial with the chief on the stand, Crawford's lawyers agreed to send the municipal court transcripts to the county court and conduct the trial on motions.

Harrington had also filed a civil suit in federal court in Waco, alleging the Crawford police had subjected his clients—a church secretary, a middle school teacher, an AmeriCorps volunteer, an employee of the nonprofit Texas Criminal Justice Coalition, and a Crawford peace activist—to illegal arrest and had violated their First Amendment rights. The suit was dismissed pending the outcome of the criminal trial. When the county court at law judge overturned all five guilty verdicts, Harrington refiled his civil suit. Judge Michael Smith, a Ronald Reagan appointee to the federal bench, quickly ruled in favor of Harrington's clients.

The conservative federal judge had little choice. Crawford had all but admitted guilt by repealing its unconstitutional parade and protest ordinance. A state judge had overturned all five guilty verdicts reached under the statute. And the constitutional "right-to-assemble and free-speech" issues were clear. Each defendant was awarded $10,000 and the city was required to pay $84,000 in legal fees—a big bite out of Crawford's municipal budget. Crawford was also stuck with the tab for the private counsel brought in to help the city attorney through the three trials.

Beyond the cost was collateral damage to Crawford's bruised reputation. The *Houston Chronicle* reported that, four months before the big bust, the Texas town had gone begging for help protecting the first family. Two cities in Delaware and one in Massachusetts had responded, donating a used ambulance, a used fire rescue truck, and a 1960s vintage fire engine. The president's hometown was taking handouts from northeastern liberal states—in other words, states where individuals and corporations are taxed to pay for essential services—anathema in Texas. We were a low-tax state with meager government services long before George Bush was governor. As governor, Bush made a poor state poorer, cutting into the revenue that would have funded police and fire services and ordering a rare budget surplus "returned to the taxpayers who know how to spend their hard-earned money better than the government does."

But the real bad news for Crawford was the gradual understanding that the free-speech zone behind the football stadium was moot. Federal judge Michael Smith inadvertently killed it when he ruled in favor of Harrington's plaintiffs. By denying Crawford cops the right to deny citizens free speech, Judge Smith started the entire county down a slippery slope toward the unencumbered free expression guaranteed by the First Amendment. "We expanded the free-speech zone to the entire county," Harrington said. "We brought McLennan County under the purview of the Bill of Rights."

Suddenly, free speech was happening everywhere. In the summer after Harrington's plaintiffs prevailed in federal court, antiwar activist and Gold Star mother Cindy Sheehan acquired a small parcel of land near the Bush ranch and turned it into "Camp Casey"—a protest encampment dedicated to the memory of her son who was killed in Iraq. Sue Niederer (see Chapter 1), whose son Seth Dvorin died in Iraq, came down from New Jersey to join the protest. Jim Harrington drove up from Austin to monitor the situation. He found McLennan County sheriff's deputies doing their own monitoring—to ensure no one's First Amendment rights were violated. Protesters remained in Camp Casey for the duration of the president's August vacation.

The political theater Jim Harrington described was Texas Grand Guignol, complete with Gendarme Flageolet and the requisite grisly conclusion that included garroting the framers of the Constitution.

The big trial in Crawford had been a laugh riot. Yet five American citizens had been arrested, tried, and convicted for driving through an American town. Veterans of the civil rights movement in this country have been down this road (some never made it back). They can explain what life is like when the Constitution provides no safety net.

In President Bush's hometown, that safety net disappeared. In a nation that claims the first written constitution establishing rule of law over rule of man, a small-town cop carved out a constitutional exclusion zone. Not only was the rule of man displacing the rule of law, but it was the rule of one man backed by a jury that had no interest in reconciling local law with the Constitution of the United States.

The Constitution was vindicated only because a public-interest law firm, defending something larger than five clients guilty of exercising their free-speech rights, went to court.

Not all First Amendment violations are so sweetly vindicated.

On October 24, 2002, Brett Bursey stood on the side of the road outside the Columbia, South Carolina, airport, holding a NO MORE WAR FOR OIL sign and waiting for President Bush to arrive. Two Secret Service agents, an airport police officer, and a state trooper approached him. One of the federal agents told Bursey he could (1) go home; (2) get in line [to see the president] if he had a ticket; (3) go to the designated demonstration area; or (4) suffer the consequences of being arrested.

Bursey picked option number 4.

He would not be moved unless they moved him.

Bursey was standing on both public property and a thirty-year-old legal precedent. He knew he was right even as airport police sergeant James Campbell handcuffed him, loaded him into a police van, and took him to the county jail. Thirty years earlier, while protesting a visit of President Richard Nixon, Bursey had been arrested on the same road and convicted on the same charge. The South Carolina Supreme Court had overturned his trespassing conviction. Bursey told the Secret Service agents and airport cop that, since the state supreme court decided *South Carolina v. Hanapole* in 1970, there is no such thing as a state trespass charge on public property. (It does seem like something of an oxymoron if you are the public.)

Jailers at the Lexington County jail handed Bursey an orange jumpsuit and told him they'd been instructed not to send him to the afternoon arraignment; he wouldn't be arraigned until the following day. Overnight detention is extreme by Lexington County standards, at least for a sober misdemeanor defendant who resided and owned property in the county. On the following afternoon, Bursey was charged with trespassing, arraigned, and released on a personal recognizance bond.

Brett Bursey isn't a virgin.

At fifty-four, the amiable and persistent activist with graying hair pulled back into a short ponytail was well known in local law enforcement circles. The October 2002 visit was Bush's third trip to South Carolina. Brett Bursey was there waiting for the president each time. He had protested the visits of the six presidents who preceded Bush—that would be every president to hold office since LBJ. In the early seventies, he served two years in jail for painting HELL NO, WE WON'T GO on the wall of his draft board. When he was arrested at the airport in 2002, he was the director of the South Carolina Progressive Network and about as close as one gets to being a full-time professional dissenter.

Brett Bursey might be the Gunga Din of presidential protest in the Carolinas.

He was not, however, guilty of trespassing.

When other dissidents arriving at the airport saw Bursey handcuffed and walking to the police van, they retreated to the designated free-speech zone about a half mile from where the president was speaking.

"Primarily, this is about clearing dissent from the camera shot," said Bursey's attorney, Lewis Pitts. "So the message communicated through the land is that everybody here is part of the cheering masses supporting the president."

Lewis described a "Barney Fife plan" used by the Secret Service and White House Advance Team. "The feds come to town a couple of days ahead of the president's visit and they bring in the local police. Then the Secret Service gets Barney all jacked up about how patriotic this is. 'We got to defend our president,' they say. And they actually tell them, don't let anyone that's protesting be anywhere but in a free-speech zone. 'We're all Americans and want people to protest and we're giving them their own separate place to do it.'

"If you're the general public and you're a fan, you're allowed in. If you're not a fan, they do what they did in Brett's case. They send in Barney Fife and Barney says you're going to be arrested for trespassing or subject to a disorderly conduct order."

Then Barney's left behind in Mayberry, holding a criminal defendant on charges that won't stand up in court. "The Secret Service and the president fly off," Pitts said. "So there's no federal trace of repression. What you've got maybe is a little fight between Barney Fife and the local ACLU. Which looks a lot less totalitarian."

Secret Service agent Holly Abel didn't go with the Mayberry metaphor, yet what she told the judge suggests Pitts is onto something: "That's just something we usually do. It facilitates the whole process if local law enforcement handles it as opposed to us. . . . That way if the locals are handling the arrest, we won't be coming back to South Carolina to testify and fill out paperwork."

It took the "locals" five months to drop the state trespass charges against Brett Bursey. They finally came around to what he told them when they handcuffed him in October: the South Carolina Supreme Court had established thirty years earlier that there is no such crime as trespassing on public property.

That's where the story would normally have ended.

But as soon as state trespass charges were dropped, U.S. attorney J. Strom Thurmond, Jr., filed federal criminal charges. Bursey was the first person ever prosecuted under USC Title 18 Section 1752(a)(1)(ii). The statute was passed in response to the JFK assassination and makes "entering or remaining in an area the Secret Service has restricted for the security of the president of the United States" a federal misdemeanor.

Bursey requested a jury trial. But because the charge was a misdemeanor, he was tried before a federal magistrate.

Magistrate judge Bristow Marchant had little sympathy for Lewis Pitts's argument that his client wasn't warned that he was in a restricted presidential zone and that the zone was not clearly marked. Bursey had been told to move by federal and state police, even if they didn't tell him he was violating a federal law. The statute under which Bursey was charged requires cordoning off restricted areas—in this case roughly one hundred acres around the airport. Judge Marchant ruled that law enforcement officers posted at the ends of the road directing traffic, and bicycle racks set up to mark a perimeter, were a cordon.

Nor did the fact situation work in Bursey's favor. He testified that there were hundreds of people standing in line to get into the hangar while he was being arrested and that many of them carried pro-Bush signs. He also said the airport police officer told him he was being arrested because he was carrying an anti-Bush sign. A Secret Service agent, a South Carolina Law Enforcement Division officer, and the airport cop contradicted Bursey's testimony. Under oath, each of them testified that the area was shut down, no one was in the president's line of sight, and Bursey's sign was never an issue.

A trial is a swearing match, and Brett Bursey lost. The federal magistrate found "more than sufficient evidence . . . to establish that Bursey had the requisite specific intent to violate 18 U.S.C. 1752(a)(1)(ii)." Bursey faced a maximum five-thousand-dollar fine and six months in prison. Judge Marchant was lenient, observing that Bursey had demonstrated no intent to harm the president and fining him five hundred dollars.

Bursey said he regrets he had no videotape of his arrest to impeach the credibility of police and Secret Service testimony. Pitts insists the trial turned on the false witness of the cops and federal agents. It wouldn't be the first time a law enforcement officer lied under oath. In fact, charges against defendants arrested in mass roundups near the end of Nixon's second term were dismissed because the ACLU dispatched videographers to document what actually happened—which didn't square with what police said happened.

But let's assume the witnesses for the government got the facts right and Brett Bursey was doing what many criminal defendants do: telling a version of the truth he hoped would exonerate him. That doesn't explain why the U.S. attorney reached for a statute enacted thirty years earlier and never before used—not even when Richard Nixon was routinely surrounded by angry protesters and the memory of the Kennedy assassination that had informed the passage of the law was so fresh it was painful. Pitts, who has practiced law in South Carolina since about the time Strom Thurmond, Jr., was born, has a theory.

Karl Rove had gone forum shopping.

Pitts believes the president's senior adviser (who dodged a subpoena when Pitts tried to have him served in Washington) saw an opportunity to apply a federal statute that would create a protest-free zone around the president. If they could pull it off in the Fourth Circuit, they would create a legal precedent that would put the statute in play across the country.

"They did this in what they knew was their home court, South Carolina, with Strom Thurmond, Jr., as United States attorney and Senator Strom Thurmond's appointees on the federal bench," Pitts said. "The Fourth Circuit is the most conservative appeals bench in the country."

The case did go up the appeals ladder, first to a district court judge, who affirmed the magistrate's decision. "The district judge said this is an era of terrorist plots and terrorist bombings," Pitts said. "That's the context that they were thinking about and even made reference to." At the court of appeals, the presiding judge on the Fourth Circuit panel opened the hearing by saying: "This is an uncommonly silly prosecution." Then she voted with the majority to uphold the ruling against Bursey.

When the U.S. Supreme Court refused to hear the case, as Pitts sees it, Karl Rove and Attorney General John Ashcroft achieved their objective. They gamed the legal system and won an appellate court review of a draconian law that would silence dissent wherever the president traveled. They have a license to arrest anyone carrying a sign or wearing a T-shirt authorities find offensive and to corral dissidents in small redoubts where they are free to exercise their First Amendment rights.

Strom Thurmond, Jr., who moved on to a private law practice in South Carolina after four years as U.S. attorney, says his decision was made with no input from Washington. "I made the decision to prosecute Mr. Bursey after consultation with my management team, the prosecutors assigned to the case, and the United States Secret Service, and no one else. . . . Although the charge levied against Mr. Bursey was a misdemeanor, the charge reaffirmed the important premise that no citizen should be permitted to disregard lawful orders of Secret Service agents whose duty is to protect the president of the United States." Thurmond added that Bursey's case was heard in three federal courts in South Carolina and his appeal turned down by the U.S. Supreme Court.

In other words, Brett Bursey, with his First Amendment complaint, was a three-time loser.

Case closed.

The Bush administration wasn't the first to suppress dissent in this country. Confiscating signs and rounding up protesters was a fairly common practice during Richard Nixon's second term. (It reached a disturbing excess when an assistant attorney general named William Rehnquist justified the arrest of thirteen thousand antiwar protesters in Washington in 1971 by declaring something he creatively described as "qualified martial law.") Police also harassed protesters during the eight years Ronald Reagan was in the White House, and to some extent during Bill Clinton's presidency.

But the Bush administration goes at it with an unprecedented totalitarian zeal. Bush operatives were mugging the First Amendment even before William Rehnquist's Supreme Court shut down the Florida recount and called the 2000 election. As part of their agreement to hold the national convention in Philadelphia in August 2000, the Republican Party demanded a two-week lease on all public property. By temporarily taking title to the streets and other public places, Bush political operatives could limit dissent to a "protest pit" a safe distance from the South Philadelphia sports complex where the convention was held. Protesters were required to apply for permits to enter the designated area for fifteen minutes of unrestricted free speech. When political free speech occurred outside the designated area, Philadelphia police stopped it, often using phalanxes of mounted officers to herd and corral protesters.

It was inspired repression of free speech, more than a year before the terrorist attacks of 9/11 and at a time when George W. Bush couldn't tell al-Qaeda from Al Pacino. And it caught on. Early on in the country's first Public Relations Presidency, the Secret Service began working to ensure that no offensive signs or placards would ever be tolerated in the presence of the president. The notion that the Bush-Cheney administration's assault on the Bill of Rights was a response to the terrorist attacks of September 2001 doesn't square with the historical record.

At Brett Bursey's trial, Lewis Pitts introduced trial transcripts from two other states where defendants were prosecuted for essentially "carrying a sign that might offend the president." The first sign arrest was made two months after George W. Bush delivered his January 2001 maiden inaugural address, when he visited Western Michigan University in Kalamazoo. Waiting for him was Antoine Jennings. A political science major in his senior year, Jennings carried a sign that read WELCOME TO WESTERN MICHIGAN, *GOVERNOR* BUSH. Perhaps the young African American student got course credit for the lesson the Bush entourage provided him on the power of the executive branch. And the diminished function of the First Amendment.

Jennings was confronted by WMU police, arrested, and charged with trespassing. In an interview later the same day, he told a reporter that a campus police officer informed him he was being placed under arrest because he was carrying a protest sign.

In this excerpt from Jennings's trial, Campus police captain Wesley Carpenter leaves no doubt about what got the WMU senior booked, mugged, and fingerprinted on the campus he had called home for four years.

Carpenter is being questioned by Jennings's attorney.

> Q: And what did you and the Secret Service do to prepare for the President's arrival?
>
> A: They arrived approximately three days prior to his arrival, and we set up the established area surrounding inside and outside of the facility for the security of the arrival of the President. They established areas that public were not allowed to enter. They established areas for demonstrators. They established areas for the press, the news media and the public who had—ticket holders to actually enter the venue. . . . And we had specific instructions from the Secret Service that any demonstrators would have to demonstrate from that established area.
>
> Q: And, again, what did the defendant say to this?

A: He became argumentative and wanted to argue about if he could—why he couldn't go into there and that it was his campus, and he kept saying, you're only doing this because I'm carrying a sign or I'm demonstrating, and I kept telling him that this was a secured area, and it was for the protection of the President, and he had to comply with the rules that had been sent up by the Secret Service.

Q: Okay. And so they could have stayed on the south side of Oliver Street? That was all open to the public?

A: As long as they weren't demonstrating.

Q: Ah. And that—that gets to the heart of the matter, I guess.

A: Right.

Q: This was all open to the public here (indicating)?

A: Correct.

Q: And anybody could have gone down to this area (indicating) and stood and watched—

A: Yes.

Q: —the President?

A: Yes.

Q: But what happens if somebody comes into this area and they hold up a sign?

A: If it's on sticks or wooden—anything that could be used as a weapon, then they have to go back to the demonstration area. They're not allowed to bring them down there into that area.

Q: And a sign without a stick?

A: It was my understanding the Secret Service said all demonstrators had to be in this area (indicating).

Q: So, even if they don't—

A: That were—that were—that was our instructions.

Q: Even if they don't have sticks—

A: Correct.

Q: —they can't go in the area that's otherwise open to the public?

A: That was the instructions we were given.

Q: And a sign without a stick is no threat to anyone, is it?

A: That's correct.

Q: Okay. But the Secret Service didn't want anybody—and this was your understanding and the rule that you were enforcing—

A: Exactly.

Q: —nobody who was critical of the President could be seen in this area; they had to go behind the building?

A: That's correct.

Q: And this was an order that you—or not an order—this was the request of the Secret Service?

A: It was an order of the Secret Service.

Pitts also introduced the transcript of the trial of retired steelworker Bill Neel in Coraopolis, Pennsylvania. Neel, sixty-six, and his sister had been standing with a large group of Bush supporters lined up along a residential street in Neville Island, Pennsylvania, waiting for the presidential motorcade. Neel didn't quite fit in with Bush admirers holding up signs that read WE ❤ BUSH, GOD BLESS U.S., GO GEORGE!

County detective John Ianachione spotted Neel's THE BUSHES MUST LOVE THE POOR—THEY'VE MADE SO MANY OF US sign and told him to take it to the free-speech zone. During Bush's Labor Day 2001 visit to Pennsylvania, free speech was allowed on a baseball field where protesters stood behind a chain-link fence out of sight of the president. Neel refused. He was handcuffed and arrested, and his sign was confiscated. His sister had no protest sign, but when she protested her brother's arrest, she was arrested with him.

Both were charged with disorderly conduct.

Neel's trial began with Detective Ianachione telling Judge Shirley R. Trkula how he came to arrest John Neel and his sister Joyce Lynn Neel:

> Magistrate Trkula: Okay, Detective, let me hear what you have to say.
>
> The Witness: Yes, Your Honor. On September 2nd, President Bush was coming to town, and over on Neville Island there, and I was assigned to a uniformed detail, and I was specifically assigned to the firehouse area along the main route of travel into town. There was an assembly permit established for the memorial park area for protesters at that site. My duties were pretty much to guide protesters into the assembly area, made sure that all the protesters went into the assembly area. It's a large fenced-in baseball field.
>
> Magistrate Trkula: Who applied for the permit? The protesters—
>
> The Witness: It was the protest group, yes.
>
> Magistrate Trkula: —applied for the permit—
>
> The Witness: Yes, Your Honor . . .

Magistrate Trkula: Okay. So does that mean all protesters had to go in the park?

The Witness: Yes. That was my—

Magistrate Trkula: If they belonged to that group. What if they didn't belong to that group? What if they lived on the island?

The Witness: Well, it was my understanding if they were exhibiting themselves as a protester, they were to go in that area.

Magistrate Trkula: Who told you that?

The Witness: My supervisors.

Magistrate Trkula: Okay.

The Witness: And also the Secret Service. Like I said, I was there. We were guiding— All the protesters went in except for Mr. Neel and his sister at that time, Joyce Lynn Neel. They were asked numerous times over and over to go into the area. They were exhibiting this sign here. . . . But anyways, we continued to, you know, ask them to go in there. They refused. They were arrested at that point. They were taken right into the adjacent firehouse, and myself and Detective Mett sat there with Mr. Neel and Mrs. Neel until the President was done and he left town.

Neel's lawyer, Thomas J. Farrell, followed Judge Trkula, cross-examining the defendant.

Q. But your directions were only those folks with signs critical of the President needed to be in the protest area?

A. Yes, sir, people as I would understand to be in protest.

Q. Okay. And you were given those directions by who?

A. My direct chain of command was Sergeant Gorcheck and the Secret Service. I'm sorry, I don't know the names of the Secret Service.

Q. Were you at a meeting before [September] 2nd with the Secret Service?

A. There was a brief meeting. People were detailed to different areas and it was explained the assembly area was there, and the people protesting were to go into the assembly area where there was a permit obtained for that area for that purpose.

Q. And you were told that by both Sergeant Gorcheck and the Secret Service at this briefing before the protest?

A. Yes, sir.

Q. Okay. And you say the Secret Service. Was it the Secret Service or were these folks White House staff? Do you know?

A. Primarily, as I understood, they were Secret Service that gave the briefing.

Q. Did they identify themselves as being from the Secret Service?

A. Yes, sir.

Fifteen minutes into the trial, the judge interrupted Farrell's cross-examination and began to question the detective. Judge Trkula had seen a news photo of a local woman enthusiastically awaiting Bush's arrival and wanted to know why Neel was treated differently. When the detective said Neel was singled out because he was "in protest," the judge stopped the proceeding.

> Magistrate Trkula: Okay. All right. Yeah, I understand. I understand where you're coming from, and I understand where you're coming from, because it's a critical time. And I guess because of 9/11 they're a little more careful than before.
>
> But I do not believe that this rises to the charge of disorderly conduct. And I believe this is America, and that's why our forefathers came here, for freedom of speech. And I don't— Once you stop that, whatever happened to "I may not agree with what you say, but I'll defend to my death your right to say it"?
>
> The Witness: Your Honor, I was just—
>
> Magistrate Trkula: So I'll dismiss this, and good luck to you [Neel]. And maybe the next time find a different way to protest. I don't know. So you don't have to end up in here.

Charges against Joyce Lynn Neel were also dropped, and Detective Ianachione walked across the courtroom and handed Bill Neel his sign, which had been confiscated and locked in an evidence vault.

The Neels got a better deal than Brett Bursey because there was no federal statute deployed against Bill Neel. And because the arrest of a sixty-six-year-old man for standing on a public street with a sign that might offend the president engaged the gag reflex of a judge who didn't even feel compelled to cite the Constitution to rule that this sort of repression has no place in a democracy.

Most Americans won't be shocked to read that the Secret Service is secretive—even if the earpieces and sunglasses are a giveaway. But Secret Service secrecy is expected to serve the purpose of protecting the president of the United States, not violate First Amendment rights of citizens of the United States. Though they did Lewis Pitts no good in federal court, the transcripts he introduced are on-the-record-under-oath accounts of Secret Service agents ordering local police officers to arrest dissenters engaged in constitutionally protected free speech. (In a country founded by dissenters.)

Pitts even found agents breaking their own rules. A U.S. Secret Service procedures manual section entitled "Demonstrations" stipulates: "In the absence of specific fact or observable actions which would indicate a demonstration may pose a risk to a USSS protectee, protected facility, or to public safety, demonstrators are to be treated as members of the general public."

That's unequivocal bureaucratic English. Not as eloquent as the First Amendment, but complying with it in letter and spirit.

The paper trail Lewis Pitts turned up suggests that all roads lead to Rome. So Secret Service policy isn't likely to change until the emperor returns to his ranch in Texas. In fact, it will get worse. In December 2005, Senator Arlen Specter made a technical adjustment to the revised USA Patriot Act. The provision the moderate Republican from Pennsylvania inserted with no debate seems to render moot the federal misdemeanor charge for which Brett Bursey was prosecuted. Henceforth, anyone caught in a restricted zone will now be subject to *felony* charges under the Patriot Act, punishable by one year in jail and a fine. "Restricted zones" will include National Special Security Events—such as the Olympics, the Super Bowl, and any one of President Ronald Reagan's many funerals. The zones—themselves designated as protectees—can be shut down for days before and after the president's scheduled arrival.

No reasonable American would oppose increased security for places and events that are likely terrorist targets. Congress identified 160 potential sites for terrorist attacks in 2003. By 2005 there were 77,769 possible targets. Not all were National Special Security Events or sites. But for an administration that has criminalized dissent, each of them—including the Illinois Apple and Pork Festival—is an enforcement opportunity.

But no reasonable American who understands the Bill of Rights would support the novel defense of two private security guards who threw a couple out of a Bush Social Security Town Hall in 2005 in Denver because they arrived in a car with a NO BLOOD FOR OIL sticker on the bumper.

"The president may constitutionally make viewpoint-based exclusionary determinations in convening his own message," the attorneys representing the Republican Party volunteers who threw the couple out of the president's forum said in court filings. "So in following the instructions of the White House, [the security guards who escorted the couple from the taxpayer-supported Bush event] did not violate any of the plaintiffs' constitutional rights."

Viewpoint-based exclusionary determinations?

It's a concept.

But not one that the framers of the Constitution would have recognized.

THREE

The Kids Are Alright

"Congress shall make no law . . . abridging the freedom . . . of the press." Our framers did this for a reason. There are countries today where journalists are punished and imprisoned for reporting on their government. If anyone here wants to imprison journalists, I invite them to spend some time in China, Cuba, or North Korea and see whether they feel safer.

—Representative Jane Harman, May 25, 2006

Kill a chicken to scare the monkeys.

—Chinese proverb

On the morning of May 8, 2007, Joshua Wolf was one of six federal inmates in handcuffs and jailhouse jumpsuits walking from the Bureau of Prisons shuttle to the garage entrance of the Phillip Burton Federal Building on Golden Gate Avenue in San Francisco. The bus had made the thirty-five-mile trip in from the Federal Corrections Institute at Dublin, where Wolf was serving his 199th day in custody. He was doing soft time (Dublin is minimum security) on a federal taillight rap.

It's a complicated story.

Wolf had not spent 199 days in jail for breaking a forty-five-dollar taillight lens on a San Francisco police squad car. He was, in fact, charged with no crime. He's a blogger and freelance news videographer. On July 8, 2005, he was covering an Anarchist Action protest in San Francisco. Although no one was ever brought to trial, several crimes were committed as bands of masked anarchists marched and ran through the Mission District. Most of what happened was political vandalism. Store and office windows were splashed with paint. Newspaper racks were thrown onto the streets. Cars and buses were covered with graffiti. A taillight on a police car was broken. But San Francisco police officer Peter Shields was hit on the back of the head and suffered a severe skull fracture.

Breaking windows, refusing to disperse, painting graffiti on buses, and blocking city streets are punishable by fines and jail time. Physically assaulting a police officer is deadly serious. But none of these actions constitutes a federal offense, and no one claimed Wolf had committed any crime, state or federal. The charges against the demonstrators who assaulted the police officer were filed in state court.

That's why the broken taillight is important. Like most American cities, San Francisco receives federal grants to spend on law enforcement. Some of that money is spent on equipment, such as police cruisers. The local police initially claimed a protester had tried to burn a police car. But what was burning was a piece of Styrofoam ignited by a firecracker. An arson charge might not stick, so the taillight became the hook to bring in the feds.

Wolf was surprised when an FBI agent in a Hawaiian shirt, shorts, and sandals showed up at his door three days after the protest. Two city cops and another agent quickly joined the Hawaiian undercover act and demanded all Wolf's video outtakes and names of subjects at the protest. Wolf told them he had witnessed no assault on a police officer. Short segments of the video he'd sold to NBC and two other local TV news outlets had already aired. He had posted longer segments on his website: joshwolf.net/blog/. His camera had been trained on the officer who jumped from his car and tackled and held a suspect on the curb—not the officer whose skull was fractured after he raced off in pursuit of another group of protesters. Wolf told the agents they were violating his First Amendment rights as a journalist.

Two hundred days for a broken taillight does seem excessive. But, as you will see, Wolf was prosecuted by a true believer working for a tough-on-crime president whose execution record as governor of Texas won't be surpassed without the aid of performance-enhancing drugs (150 men and 2 women in six years, each getting a brisk fifteen-minute, final-day review over coffee with his staff counsel Al Gonzales).

San Francisco's U.S. attorney, Kevin Ryan, who started the prosecution of Wolf, was the anomaly in the Al Gonzales–Karl Rove purge of U.S. attorneys. He was the guy who earned the right to be fired long before his eight undeserving colleagues were dismissed. A Department of Justice memo describes his failures:

- Significant management problems have manifested during his tenure.
- The district has become one of the most fractured offices in the nation.
- Morale has fallen to the point that it is harming prosecutorial efforts.
- The USA [U.S. attorney] has lost the confidence of many of his career prosecutors.

But Ryan was a member of the right-wing Federalist Society and had been praised by his superiors for following administration policies. He was "a loyal Bushie" doing the political hackwork expected of GWB's USAs even as his office unraveled around him.

Six months after FBI agents first showed up at his door, Wolf received a subpoena. Not your garden-variety grand jury subpoena, which would have originated in San Francisco. The San Francisco police were using a broken taillight to bring to bear on a lefty blogger the high-caliber investigative firepower we're all counting on to prevent, say, another terrorist flying a commercial airliner into a tall building. The subpoena served on Josh Wolf was issued by a Joint Terrorism Task Force in Washington and would have to pertain to a rather serious federal crime and, you would think, terrorism.

Wolf's February 2006 subpoena ordered him to deliver his unedited video and his camera to a federal grand jury in San Francisco and to appear for questioning under oath. When he refused, the assistant U.S. attorney went to a federal magistrate and then to a district judge. Both judges ordered Wolf to hand over his videotapes and answer the grand jury's questions.

Wolf said no.

At a March hearing, he submitted an affidavit explaining his position to the court:

> In seeking my testimony and unpublished material, the federal government is turning me into their de facto investigator. My journalistic activities will be blighted, my reporter-subject relationship of trust with alleged anarchist protestors will be eviscerated. Protestors will refuse to speak with me and will deny me access to cover demonstrations. . . . The government's subpoena is driving a wedge between my First Amendment activities and protestors exercising their right to lawfully

> assemble by instilling fear that the government will use my documentation to catalogue and investigate individuals participating in civil dissent.

Wolf ended up in the courtroom of federal judge William Alsup, a Bill Clinton appointee that Martin Garbus, a distinguished First Amendment lawyer and one of Wolf's attorneys, describes as a "long-ball hitter"—a judge who hands out long sentences. Besides being a long-ball hitter, Judge Alsup is something of a hard-ass. He smacked down Wolf's attorney Mark Vermeulen, ending in midsentence his argument about a reporter's First Amendment rights.

"I was a law clerk on the Supreme Court when this very issue was decided against you on that," said the judge. "The U.S. Supreme Court said there is no journalist newsman's privilege under the First Amendment." When Vermeulen persisted, Alsup threatened to call in the marshals. Then he turned to the defendant—who wasn't exactly a defendant because he was charged with no crime.

Wolf offered to turn his unedited video over to the judge to view in camera and verify that no incident of arson or assault on a police officer was on the outtakes. Alsup ordered Wolf to turn the videos over to the grand jury and answer the grand jurors' questions.

"Mr. Wolf, if you don't answer the question [asked by the grand jury], you'll be subject to being put in jail until you answer the question. And or fines or lots of other possible penalties."

Assistant U.S. attorney Jeffrey Finigan added a coloratura note: "And that could be, Your Honor, for the life of the grand jury."

Wolf knew the grand jury's term wouldn't end until July 2007, with a possible six-month extension. He had done the math and was looking at as much as eighteen months in federal prison.

"Remember that lady, Miss— The journalist, Judith Miller?" the judge asked. "She was in jail a long time . . ."

When Ben Rosenfeld, another of Wolf's attorneys, tried to explain his client's constitutional protections, the judge cut him off, too. "No. I know the law. And at the contempt meeting you can bring up any other arguments that you want. Meanwhile, your client may be in jail."

At the contempt hearing, Alsup ordered Wolf locked up in the federal facility at Dublin. The Ninth Circuit Court of Appeals upheld the decision, and Wolf would best Judy Miller's 85-day record by 114 days in jail before his first (failed) attempt at mediation, in March 2007.

To U.S. attorney Kevin Ryan and agents on the JTTF, Josh Wolf must have looked like low-hanging fruit. Judy Miller had served eighty-five days on the other coast for refusing to deliver her notes and sources in the Scooter Libby investigation. But she had the institutional support and deep pockets of *The New York Times*, which paid $2 million for her legal defense. And her jailhouse visitors' log read like the Saturday night reservation book at TenPenh, the elegant Washington, D.C., restaurant. Josh Wolf was out there on a shoeshine and smile. As a blogger and freelancer, he wasn't universally accepted as a journalist. His left-wing Indymedia connections eroded his credibility among some mainstream reporters and editors. To defend himself in federal court, he needed the help of friends, the kindness of strangers, and the generosity of civil rights lawyers. He was the perfect target for an administration that wants reporters out of the way so it can create its own reality.

The balls-to-the-wall pursuit of Josh Wolf illustrates the excess of the Bushies' programmatic assault on the press. Republicans still controlled the House when the House Intelligence Committee held a rare open meeting on March 26, 2006. The larger story was lost in headlines about the lockdown of the Capitol after a false alarm that shots had been fired.

California Democrat Jane Harman warned that the framers of the Constitution ensured that "Congress shall make no law abridging the freedom of the press" for a reason. "If anyone here wants to imprison journalists, I invite them to spend some time in China, Cuba, or North Korea, and see whether they feel safer." Her concern was an administration campaign and a determination in Congress to use the threat of jailhouse jumpsuits to housebreak journalists the administration believed were getting in the way of G. W. Bush's War on Terror.

At the March 26 meeting, committee chair Peter Hoekstra was flogging Attorney General Alberto Gonzales's plan to use the Espionage Act of 1917 to prosecute reporters. It was a hollow, reckless threat. The World War I Congress that passed the Espionage Act rejected provisions Woodrow Wilson included in the act that would have criminalized publication of material declared off-limits by the president. Opponents of Wilson's draconian measures called them "un-American" and "an instrument of tyranny" and struck them from the bill. Never the sort of lawyer to be discouraged by legislative intent, Gonzales saw in one section of the Espionage Act language that, if loosely construed, might be used to jail reporters under certain circumstances. (That's the kind of syntax you get into when you write about this guy.)

The attorney general who earned his chops in the Vinson & Elkins Real Property Section in Houston wasn't threatening to turn the Espoinage Act on just any journalist. He was hot for Eric Lichtblau and James Risen of *The New York Times* and Dana Priest of *The Washington Post*. The *Times* had revealed that the National Security Agency was secretly (and illegally) listening in on domestic phone calls without warrants. At the *Post*, Priest had reported on clandestine "black site" CIA prisons in Europe (also illegal). The attorney general President Bush playfully calls Fredo—Vito

Corleone's feckless second son in *The Godfather*—wasn't going to let the letter of the law protect three treasonous reporters. If he couldn't prosecute under the Espionage Act, he could use it to warn reporters "I know where you live." Distinguished for his obsequious devotion to his boss, Fredo Gonzales was taking the fight to reporters and editors of the big, institutional press.

The Boss was out in front of his AG, even if he wasn't parsing passages in the Espionage Act. "My personal opinion is that it was a shameful act for somebody to disclose this very important program in a time of war," Bush said of the *Times*. "The fact that we're disclosing this program is helping the enemy. I can say that if somebody from al-Qaeda is calling you, we'd like to know why."

With the AG threatening to lock up reporters under a willfully misinterpreted section of a hundred-year-old statute, the president was implying that the *Times*'s reporters were guilty of treason—for revealing his clandestine violation of the law "in a time of war."

In such a spot, the man G. W. Bush playfully calls "Vice" couldn't be far behind. Dick Cheney called the *Times* story "very damaging" and said the NSA's secret surveillance program had saved thousands of American lives. He was deeply offended because the *Times* had won a Pulitzer for its reporting on the agency's illegal surveillance. "What is doubly disturbing for me," he declared, "is that not only have they gone forward with these stories, but they have been rewarded for it. For example, in the case of the Terrorist Surveillance Program by being awarded the Pulitzer Prize for outstanding journalist. I think that's a disgrace."

Bush's handpicked CIA director, Porter Goss, jumped on Gonzales's threats of criminal prosecution: "I've called the FBI and the Department of Justice. It is my aim, and it is my hope, that we will witness a grand jury investigation with reporters present, being asked to reveal who is leaking [classified] information," Goss told the Senate Intelligence Committee.

For Republicans who held the First Amendment in low regard (that would be a majority in the Congress), it was open season on reporters.

Kentucky senator Jim Bunning argued that the editors and reporters at the *Times* should be charged with "treason." (Treason is punishable by death.)

House Homeland Security Committee chair Peter King—once the Irish Republican Army's go-to guy in New York—accused the *Times* of aiding the enemy. "I believe the Attorney General of the United States should begin a criminal investigation and prosecution of *The New York Times*," King said. "And that it should include the writers who wrote the story, the editors who worked on it, and the publisher." King told Fox News that the criminal investigations Gonzales was planning would put reporters and editors "on the defensive, where they belong." There it was. Behind the bluster, empty threats of prosecution, and accusations of treason was a campaign to intimidate the press.

The New York Times and *The Washington Post* have institutional footings that allow them to stand up to a president. Smaller papers that would crack under pressure from the White House, or fold before putting up $2 million (or $25,000) to defend a reporter, got the message. The U.S. attorney investigating Scooter Libby had opened the floodgates (or prison gates) by jailing Judith Miller. Now the AG was making jail for journalists national policy. The president, vice president, and Republican majority in Congress joined the fight with the sort of zeal we hadn't seen since George Bush and Bill Frist tried to resurrect Terri Schiavo. Reporters would know there's a price to be paid for revealing state secrets. Publishers and editors would get the message.

Arizona Republican Rick Renzi—who might yet achieve the distinction of being both the most piss-witted *and* the most corrupt member of Congress—was one of the more queerly inarticulate foot soldiers in the war on the press. Prosecuting journalists,

Renzi told his colleagues on the committee, would have the "chilling effect of a sword to a glacier." Renzi couldn't quite recall Georgetown professor Jon Turley's warning of "a Sword of Damocles" hanging over reporters' heads. But he knew there was a sword in there somewhere and that it was time to chill. "I believe that the attorney general and that the president should use all the powers of existing law to begin to bring criminal charges," said the congressman.

By the end of the Bush administration's spring campaign against the *Times*, 60 percent of those surveyed by Fox News said that the newspaper did more to help terrorist groups by publishing the NSA story. Only 27 percent said the story did more to help the public. Forty-three percent said the paper was guilty of treason. It was an odd response, if typical of Fox's skewed polling, considering that the administration had broken the law. Somehow the president and his vice president had convinced the public that reporters were aiding and abetting terrorists.

It was in this climate that Josh Wolf became a First Amendment prisoner of conscience. Unable to intimidate the big boys at the *Times* and the *Post*, the Department of Justice turned to Josh Wolf. Reporters have a stark decision to make when told to reveal sources or hand over work product. They can obey a judge's or grand jury's order. Or they can go to jail. That was settled by a five to four vote in a 1972 Supreme Court case styled *Branzburg v. Hayes*—one of several "swords to glaciers" hanging over reporters' heads.

Paul Branzburg was a Louisville *Courier-Journal* reporter who had witnessed a drug crime in the course of writing a story and was ordered to identify the subjects. When he refused to testify and was held in contempt, the Supreme Court upheld the lower court's order. The fifth vote on the divided court was Justice Lewis Powell, who wrote a concurring opinion. Powell agreed with the majority, but he argued that the decision was limited, that "if a newsman has reason to believe that his testimony implicates confidential source relationships without a legitimate need of law enforcement, he will have access to the court and a motion to quash, and an appropriate protective order may be entered."

Powell also warned of a need to strike a balance "between the freedom of the press and the obligation of all citizens to give relevant testimony with respect to criminal conduct." Lawyers have used Powell's opinion to try to protect their journalists' sources and keep their clients out of jail. First Amendment lawyer Floyd Abrams tried to turn Powell's concurrence into a defense of Judith Miller when she was subpoenaed in the Scooter Libby case. The D.C. federal district court and the D.C. court of appeals sent Miller straight to jail—ending what Georgetown law professor Turley describes as the "intentional ambiguity" that kept prosecutors out of reporters' notebooks despite the 1972 Supreme Court ruling.

Yet despite *Branzburg*, there are valid reasons why Josh Wolf should never have been locked up.

Martin Garbus has been defending free speech since he represented comedian and social satirist Lenny Bruce in the sixties. He joined the defense team after Wolf had been in jail for more than four months. Garbus says the FBI had no business knocking on Josh Wolf's door, because there was no federal crime.

Garbus echoed Justice Powell's argument about a "newsman," who would worry that "his testimony implicates confidential source relationships without a legitimate need of law enforcement." Garbus said that while Wolf had no explicit confidentiality agreement with the anarchist protesters he was covering, the subjects who confided in him never thought he would reveal their identities to the police. Garbus also referred to Powell's argument about "striking a balance" between reporters' First Amendment rights and the obligation to testify in criminal trials.

"Here there's nothing to balance," Garbus said. "There's no

national security issue. It's not like the judge knows this guy is going to go out and blow up the World Trade Center tomorrow. He represents no threat at all. And he has no information about any threat."

If those arguments hang on the thin thread of one concurring Supreme Court opinion, the unassailable legal argument that explains why Josh Wolf never should have been imprisoned pertains to the broken taillight. California was one of more than thirty states that passed journalist shield laws after the Supreme Court's *Branzburg* decision left reporters unprotected. California's shield law, one of the strongest in the nation, provided absolute protection for Wolf, his work product, and his sources.

To get around the state law, federal prosecutors needed a federal crime. When their arson charge looked dicey, they pointed to a broken taillight, claiming the anarchists had damaged federal property. "They were groping for some justification," Garbus said. "It was an attempt to avoid the California shield law." They stretched the facts to distort the law. A state offense was federalized to bring in the al-Qaeda squad.

Garbus said the coercive detention of Wolf only makes sense in the context of the Bush administration's abuse of the criminal justice system. "There were a lot of other tapes out there and a lot of other witnesses," Garbus said. "There were better tapes that showed the cop car. But they haven't subpoenaed those tapes. And they know about them." Garbus said he believes local police, working in concert with the FBI, are bringing people in to question and subpoenaing their videos and notes to build a database.

It's a concern that other lawyers and civil libertarians are frequently raising. The Bush Department of Justice uses coercive prosecution as an extension of what should be criminal investigation. It's conduct that might be justified if the judge knew someone was "going to blow up the World Trade Center tomorrow." But too often, the Bush DOJ treats defendants it doesn't like—such as Josh Wolf—as potential bombers.

The claim that Joint Terrorism Task Forces are engaged in clandestine surveillance of American citizens is spelled out in an amicus brief the ACLU filed in support of Wolf. ACLU attorneys found FBI agents in Pittsburgh secretly investigating the Thomas Merton Center, described in bureau files as "a left wing organization advocating among other political causes, pacifism." In Denver, the JTTF had Food Not Bombs under surveillance, quietly monitoring the distribution of food to the homeless. On California campuses, the FBI was watching antiwar protesters on the UC Berkeley and Santa Cruz campuses, feeding information about their activities into a Department of Defense antiterrorism database.

On the trail of lefty do-gooders was the same federal agency that ignored its agent Coleen Rowley's desperate entreaties to investigate Zacharias Moussaoui while he was in custody prior to 9/11, and that disregarded antiterrorism agent Kenneth Williams's urgent entreaties to canvass flight schools he suspected were providing instructions to Osama bin Laden's agents (as Williams specifically wrote in a pre-9/11 memo). Antiterrorist specialists from the FBI were staking out pacifist Catholics, charitable groups feeding the homeless, and students taunting military recruiters on California campuses. And journalist Joshua Wolf.

"The very reason [the U.S. attorney] is after him is because it was an anti-Bush demonstration," Garbus said. "An antiwar demonstration. The only reason he's being selected is because of his politics."

We've been down this road before—during the administration of Richard Nixon, where Dick Cheney got his first government job. Nixon sent the black-bag squad into the office of the psychiatrist of military analyst Daniel Ellsberg to read through files after Ellsberg leaked the "Pentagon Papers."

As President Gerald Ford's chief of staff in 1974, Cheney wanted to break into the home of then *New York Times* reporter Seymour Hersh. Cheney suggested getting a search warrant "to go after Hersh's papers in his apt." "Will we get hit with violating the 1st amendment to the constitution?" he asked in a handwritten note. The future vice president wasn't concerned that the administration would be violating the First Amendment, only that it might get caught doing so.

With Cheney in charge at the White House and Fredo Gonzales running the Justice Department, fears that Wolf's incarceration was part of a coordinated surveillance campaign seem well founded.

The doors of Judge Joseph Spero's courtroom on the fifteenth floor of the Phillip Burton Federal Building were locked for most of the day on May 8, 2006. The hearing was closed to the press, who could only watch through the narrow vertical windows on the courtroom door. It commenced at 10:00 A.M. under light security. "It's just that kid who's locked up because of his videotape," said "Rover 12," one of the building's security guards, on his way out for lunch. At the counsel table sat Josh Wolf, Marty Garbus, and two attorneys from the First Amendment Project. At the head of the table sat Magistrate Judge Spero, for Wolf a welcome change from district judge William Alsup.

With expressive eyes and a thick mustache that accentuated a generous smile, Spero seemed to be joking with Wolf. Spero's brown sport coat and red bow tie (rather than black robes) improved the atmospherics Judge Alsup had created six months earlier, when he ordered Wolf locked up until he talked. Garbus had filed a Grumbles motion, one of those legal mechanisms that, like Miranda rights, memorialize a plaintiff or defendant by affixing his name to a legal procedure. A Grumbles makes the argument that detention to compel testimony has become punitive when it is evident that testimony cannot be compelled. Alsup had rejected the argument without a hearing.

Then the judge must have realized he had boxed himself in.

Wolf wasn't going submit to questioning by the grand jury and surrender his videotapes; in fact he seemed prepared to hunker down in his cell until the grand jury's term expired. So Alsup did something that Garbus had never before seen. He asked a magistrate judge to mediate the dispute and perhaps find a middle ground between Wolf and the assistant U.S. attorney working the "terrorism" case. At the mediation hearing, Wolf, with a shock of black hair, *Bye Bye Birdie* sideburns, and a sweet, sensual face, sat at the judge's left hand. His attorney sat directly in front of him. For six hours they negotiated.

In the hallway, Garbus described his client as a "lovely young man," adding, "I think he's intelligent. I've dealt with people of the right, left, and center, who in jail have become paranoid, irrational, et cetera. None of that has happened to him. He's the same kid who went in six months ago."

Assistant U.S. attorney Jeffrey Finigan was less generous. He filed an affidavit that described Wolf as a "delusional," self-styled "journalistic martyr."

At four o'clock Wolf walked out the secure back door of the courtroom. He would be back in his cell in Dublin in time for dinner. Garbus was flying back to New York to draft another Grumbles motion, to which he would attach a psychologist's report describing Wolf's emotional stability and resolve. On the following morning, Wolf began his two hundredth day in federal custody.

On Day 224, Wolf was back in Judge Spero's courtroom. He had reached an agreement. He would deliver his unedited videotape, which he immediately posted on his website. And he would answer only two questions before the judge:

- Did he know the identity of the individual Officer Peter Shields chased?
- Did he witness any attempt at arson?

He answered no to both questions and was out of jail.

Free after six months, Josh Wolf walked a half block south

from the federal building and did something that should remind us all that the kids are alright. Standing on the steps of the San Francisco City Hall, the twenty-four-year-old blogger got it pitch perfect as he quoted from William O. Douglas's prescient dissent in the *Branzburg* case:

> As the years pass, the power of the government becomes more and more pervasive. It is a power to suffocate both people and causes. Those in power, whatever their politics, want only to perpetuate it. Now that the fences of the law and the tradition that protected the press are broken down, the people are the victims. The First Amendment, as I read it, was designed precisely to prevent that tragedy. . . .
>
> The press has a preferred position in our constitutional scheme, not to enable it to make money, not to set newsmen apart as a favored class, but to bring fulfillment to the public's right to know.

FOUR

DARWIN ON TRIAL

Congress shall make no law respecting the establishing of religion or prohibiting the free exercise thereof . . .

—from the First Amendment to the United States Constitution

It reminds me of the schoolteacher who came out to my little town of Johnson City during the depression. The school board was divided on whether the earth was flat or round. The poor fellow needed a job so bad that when they asked him what he believed he told 'em "I can teach it either way."

—LYNDON JOHNSON

The idea that man is the product of evolution rather than God's hands never seemed quite right to Rick Santorum. After the Supreme Court banned the teaching of the queerly oxymoronic "creation science" in the nation's public schools, Santorum started promoting "intelligent design"—which looked suspiciously like creation science in drag. This sanitized version of creationism holds that "forms of life began abruptly through an intelligent agency, with their distinctive features already intact, fish with fins and scales, birds with feathers, beaks, and wings . . ."

While he was the Christian right's U.S. senator from Pennsylvania, Santorum even drafted a deviously neutral amendment to George W. Bush's No Child Left Behind bill, encouraging the teaching of ID in public schools. His amendment didn't make the cut, but that didn't matter to intelligent design's Christian-right supporters. The defeated amendment represented the imprimatur of the U.S. Senate. Santorum even joined the advisory board of the Thomas More Law Center, American evangelicals' public-interest law firm.

So it's appropriate that the *Darwin v. God* confrontation in the cultural wars that began when the Reverend Jerry Falwell got into bed with President Ronald Reagan occurred in a courtroom in the state Santorum represented until voters tossed him out in November 2006.

Santorum wasn't the only marquee Republican preaching the gospel of intelligent design. President George W. Bush is a Methodist—a denomination associated with moderation, particularly in Texas, where the loopier religious right is defined by firebreathers like San Antonio's Reverend John Hagee, who has proclaimed from his pulpit that Hurricane Katrina was proof that God was angry with homosexuals in New Orleans.

These Christian-right guys are good with hurricanes. At the Republican Party's state convention in Houston in 1988 (where George H. W. Bush was nominated for a presidency that we will remember as a Republican Camelot after eight years of George W. Bush), Reverend Pat Robertson reiterated his belief that his prayers had steered Hurricane Gloria away from his Virginia Beach headquarters, refusing to apologize for the death and destruction he and God had visited upon the Northern Atlantic states where they aimed the storm.

George W. Bush isn't John Hagee or Pat Robertson. But he

found Jesus in a Men's Bible Study Group—a Biblicist cult insinuated into mainstream denominations. Bush's BSG met in Midland, a right-wing oil patch redoubt where newcomers are universally welcomed with a warm West Texas "Howdy, where do you worship?"

So it was no surprise when W. Bush joined Rick Santorum, arguing that public school science teachers should "teach both sides of the controversy." The "controversy" is that simmering scientific debate over whether man was created by God or evolved from lower forms of life. There are two problems with this argument:

- In the scientific community, there is no controversy regarding evolution.
- Teaching religion in the public schools violates the separation clause in the First Amendment.

The Pennsylvania courtroom showdown over teaching "both sides of the controversy" pitted the defenders of teaching Darwin's scientific theory of evolution in high school biology classes against evangelical Christians who would supplement Darwin with the biblically inspired intelligent design. Or, as some in the anti-Darwin faction admitted in private during the trial, replace *On the Origin of Species* with the Book of Genesis.

Maybe by 2015 or 2020 Dover, Pa., pop. 1,914, will be back the way it used to be. Before school board members Alan Bonsell and Bill Buckingham decided there was too much Darwinism in the high school biology curriculum. (They had no problem with Newtonism in the physics curriculum.) Before the Dover school board voted five to four that a disclaimer must be read before any high school biology teacher could discuss evolution. Before the board fight that pitted *Of Pandas and People*, an "intelligent design" biology textbook published in Texas (it's always Texas), against the national publishing industry standard, *Biology*. Before one Christian school board member threw a chair at another for challenging his commitment to the faith that divides the twenty congregations in this Pennsylvania town.

It was in a closed meeting, when cooler heads who might have argued the practical utility of the Establishment Clause were running for the door, that chairs started flying in Dover. In a pretrial deposition, Angie Yingling described board members Noel Weinrich and Bill Buckingham's executive-session smackdown. Yingling would resign from a school board gone round the bend over the godlessness of Darwin's theory of evolution. Eric Rothschild, the Philadelphia lawyer brought in by the ACLU for the trial, questioned Yingling for her deposition.

> Angie Yingling: If you don't go along with Bill he thinks you are an atheist and questions your religion. You can't do that with Noel. Noel gets violently angry. They almost went to blows with fists. And the chairs were flying because Bill says you are an atheist and you don't go along with it.
>
> Eric Rothschild: Along with what?
>
> Angie Yingling: With him, with intelligent design. Bill thinks you don't believe in God.
>
> Eric Rothschild: Was this in executive session?
>
> Angie Yingling: Yeah. Yeah. Heather and I thought we were going to get hit [we were] right in it. And the chairs were flying right over us. We thought we were going to get punched. . . . It's really bad.
>
> Eric Rothschild: What do you recall Bill saying?
>
> Angie Yingling: Do you believe in God? I remember that. Noel just went after him, "How dare you." And Bill stood his ground . . . as sick as he is.

Eric Rothschild: What was the reaction of the other people?

Angie Yingling: Everybody is trying to get out the door. And me and Heather, we were caught right there. We were in the seats with them, which flew. The seats flew in the air.

Eric Rothschild: God or human lifted?

Angie Yingling: Both.

The question about God's hand on the folding chairs seemed like a lawyer's attempt to inject a little levity into a deposition. Until Dover Area School District superintendent Richard Nilsen took the witness stand at the October 2005 trial. Under oath Nilsen said he believes it's reasonable to teach high school biology students that the origin of life on our planet can be traced to an intelligent designer whom (or that) no one has ever seen and whom (or that) may or may not exist any longer. Or to aliens who brought some form of life here a long time ago, then returned to space or somewhere.

Nilsen had already argued in his deposition that intelligent design wasn't necessarily linked to belief in God, because aliens are another possibility that ID's proponents take into account. He admitted little knowledge about the intelligent design curriculum his board members were forcing on science teachers and said that most of his information regarding aliens came from board member Angie Yingling, who didn't subscribe to the theory but has listened to its proponents. If Yingling was Dr. Nilsen's source on aliens, he probably got something like this, as quoted from her deposition: "Just that aliens brought life forms here. In other words, there's huge universes and galaxies way bigger than ours and they finally decide to settle here. There is a name to it. I don't know the name. They have a name, the people who practice and believe that."

Superintendent Nilsen added chaos theory as another possibility but didn't elaborate. He failed to mention the "time-traveling molecular biologist" some intelligent design advocates believe introduced life to our planet.

Eric Rothschild was joking when he asked if God was tossing chairs about. Rich Nilsen was serious about aliens.

God and aliens in American high school science classes in 2004? Even in Texas, lectures about aliens bringing life to Earth are mostly relegated to late-night, local-access cable channels. That a school superintendent would take that position in a federal courtroom should give us all a greater appreciation of the wisdom of our Founding Fathers.

What mischiefs may not be dreaded?
—James Madison

Historians debate James Madison's personal religious convictions. But he arrived in New York for the First Congress of our new republic in 1789 as a devout church-and-state separationist and advocate of a separation clause in the Bill of Rights. The record is clear. Four years earlier Madison had led the fight against a Virginia statehouse tax to fund religious teaching, staking out a clear position in the "Memorial and Remonstrance" he published: "Religion or the duty which we owe to our Creator and the manner of discharging it, can be directed only by reason and conviction, not by force or violence," Madison began. "The Religion then of every man must be left to the conviction and conscience of every man."

In the fifteen points that followed, he inveighed against any government support of any religion. In fact, Madison didn't exactly embrace the idea of organized religious sects. "What influence in fact have ecclesiastical establishments had on Civil

Society?" he wrote. "In some instances they have been seen to erect a spiritual tyranny on the ruins of the Civil authority; in many instances they have been seen upholding the thrones of political tyranny; in no instance have they been seen the guardians of the liberties of the people."

Madison also warned that state support could turn Christian virtue into Christian vice. "The very appearance of the Bill has transformed 'that Christian forbearance, love and charity,' which of late mutually prevailed, into animosities and jealousies, which may not soon be appeased. What mischiefs may not be dreaded, should this enemy to the public quiet be armed with the force of a law?"

The country was fragmented among Baptists, Congregationalists, Quakers, Anglicans, Presbyterians, Unitarians, Universalists, some Catholics, and a scattering of Jews on the margins of society. Six state constitutions allowed for the establishment of multiple sects. In some cases, certain denominations were supported by taxation, making the salvation of souls a hot market. In Massachusetts, the dominant Congregationalists schemed to siphon tax support from Episcopalians, Baptists, and Quakers. In South Carolina, Baptists, Independents, Methodists, and Anglicans were sanctioned as "true Christian faiths." In New Hampshire, Quakers, Episcopalians, Presbyterians, Baptists, and other dissenters were exempt from paying tax to support the sanctioned Congregationalists. Anglicans in New York pointed to a Colonial-era law they claimed grandfathered them in as the exclusive established church. The early United States of America was a Tom Lehrer satire, lacking enough Jews to bind the Christians together in the spirit of ecumenical persecution.

What happened in Dover, Pennsylvania, 215 years after James Madison fought for a separation clause to keep church and state honest, is a cautionary tale about mixing religion and public policy.

My dad calls them whacked-out religious. . . . They are real adamant about everybody being a Christian and doing the right thing.

—from the deposition of Dover school board member ANGIE YINGLING

What lawyers call "the fact situation" in *Tammy Kitzmiller, et al. v. Dover Area School District, et al.* is straightforward enough, once you sort through fifteen file boxes of depositions, twenty-one days of testimony, and more than a thousand exhibits.

Two members of the Dover school board persuaded a majority of the board to make the high school biology curriculum more compatible with fundamentalist Christian belief. They required that students be warned that evolution is not a "fact," that it includes gaps and problems, and that a Christian-friendly version of the origin of life known as "intelligent design" provides another "scientific" alternative. They tried to approve the creationist textbook *Of Pandas and People* as a companion to the scientific biology text. When they failed, they conspired to place sixty copies of *Pandas* in the library for students to use as reference books and lied about how the books got there. They dispatched their assistant superintendent, Mike Baksa, to the county's private religious schools to search for biology textbooks compatible with the Book of Genesis and to Messiah College in nearby Grantham to explore teaching techniques. They consulted Seattle's Discovery Institute regarding the teaching of intelligent design. They sought advice from a law firm that describes itself "as the sword and shield of people of faith" and its mission as "defending the religious freedom of Christians."

Then they went after the high school faculty.

Board members questioned biology teachers about how they taught human descent and the "origin of life." They compelled science teachers to show up on Saturdays to watch videos provided by the Discovery Institute—a biblical creationist advocacy group cross-dressing as a scientific think tank. They summoned science teachers to meet with a board member who cautioned them about how evolution was taught. They warned biology teachers that one member of the board wanted a fifty-fifty split between the teaching of evolution and that of creationism. They required high school teachers to sign on to a policy that questioned the validity of the theory of evolution and to stand before their students and read a four-paragraph evolution disclaimer.

When we asked a minister on the school board what is appropriate for biology teachers to teach about the origin of life, he responded with a question: "What are the first five words in the Old Testament?"

That would be: "In the beginning God created."

There were warnings that religious fervor threatened to displace reason. One incident in 2002 suggested how bad things would become. In 1998, a graduating senior donated his class project to the high school. It was a mural depicting the ascent of man, step by step, panel by panel, walking out of his stooped hominid past into his erect *Homo sapiens* present. Custodians refused teachers' requests to hang the mural on the wall, so it sat orphaned on the chalk rail under a blackboard at the back of a biology classroom. The last weekend of summer in 2002, district grounds supervisor Larry Reeser dragged the mural to the trash pile for a private auto-da-fé. Bill Buckingham, who attended Harmony Grove Community Church with Reeser, joined him and "gleefully watched" as it burned. Buckingham's appointment to a vacant school board seat six months later would turn the board of education into a board of censors.

Bill Buckingham swore he knew nothing about the mural until after it was burned. But as we say in East Texas: "His mouth ain't a prayer book." He later showed board members a photo of the "ape genitals" he said he never wanted his grandkids to see. The genitals were a sore spot for the grounds superintendent, too. "Did you see the monkey's genitals hanging out there?" Reeser asked a *York Daily Record* reporter.

Science Department chair Bertha "Bert" Spahr is one of several genuine heroes in Dover's church-state fight. When she learned what had happened to her former student's work, she went to the superintendent. Dr. Rich Nilsen said he knew where the mural ended up but it was none of Bert's business—an early sign that the superintendent was in congregation with the religious extremists on the board.

Bill Buckingham's appointment to the school board occurred in February 2003. Another evangelical Christian was appointed along with him, and the board achieved a critical mass of what Angie Yingling's father had described as "whacked-out religious." Six of the nine board members belonged to fundamentalist congregations. More important, Buckingham joined Alan Bonsell, the owner of a radiator repair shop who seemed to devote most of his waking hours to campaigning against the biblical heresy of evolution and the absence of God in the teaching of American history.

Bonsell is an imposing man with the cocky look and demeanor of a minor-league baseball player—including the close-cropped hair, goatee, and addiction to chewing gum. His father, another devout evangelical, is also a local businessman who had previously served on the school board. Bonsell's selection by his fellow board members as president provided him additional muscle. He used it, usually behind the scenes, while Bill Buckingham openly intimidated other board members.

Bonsell had met with science teachers in the fall of 2003. They were aware that his daughter would be enrolling in biology the following semester, that he wanted a fifty-fifty split between evolution and creationism, and that he was a "young earth creationist." Young earth creationists reject scientific proof that the earth is billions of years old. Based on calculations of events in the

Book of Genesis, they have determined the earth is from five to ten thousand years old. They reject radiocarbon dating and the geologic fossil record. (A local Baptist preacher monitoring the trial explained that the fossil record was put in place by God to trick us and test our faith.)

Bonsell told the science teachers he was concerned that what students were taught in Dover High School's biology classes would contradict what they were taught by their parents. He didn't want teachers "caught in the middle," with students thinking "somebody is lying." It was a chilling message. To accommodate Bonsell's daughter and the children of other biblical literalists, science teachers would have to avoid certain topics.

This was like nothing the Dover science faculty had ever seen. They were already working in a circumscribed space. They reassured Bonsell that they taught nothing about the origins of life. They limited teaching of evolution to speciation within birds, studying the finches Darwin had studied on the Galápagos Islands. No primate-related topic was ever taught. Students asking questions about origins of life—or any "monkey to man" questions—were told to explore those issues with their parents or their pastors.

Bonsell gave the teachers his blessing, and the science faculty had dodged the bullet. Science Department chair Bert Spahr told them to continue teaching biology as they had been. They were free to teach evolution—or at least the cramped version authorized by their board, with no mention of man's common ancestry with primates. They did so through the end of the school year.

Then they heard from Bill Buckingham.

In 2004, Dover High School was overdue for a new biology textbook. In April, the science faculty settled on *Biology* by Kenneth Miller and Joseph Levine. It was a new edition of the same text Dover High teachers had used for seven years. And it's used in 35 percent of high school biology classes in the United States.

The board needed to move quickly so the books would be available when the 2004–5 school year began.

Bill Buckingham said no.

As a member of the school board's Curriculum Committee, Buckingham sent teachers his list of concerns with the biology book—which he later admitted he hadn't read. He complained that the text was "laced with Darwinism." The contents of this book—and the mural he told a group of teachers he had "gleefully watched" burn—made him wonder what science teachers were teaching.

Biology teacher Jen Miller described Buckingham's concerns. "Most of the discussion was focused around, you know, again, I thought you didn't teach origins of life, how can this mural be in the back of a classroom if you don't teach that? What message does that send to the students if you're not teaching it but this mural is in the back? And, again disagreeing with the whole idea, that man evolved, I guess, or came from monkeys."

When the biology textbook was on the agenda again at the June 14, 2004, board meeting, the apeshit hit the fan. Not since the firing of the high school football coach had so many concerned citizens turned out for a school board meeting in Dover. Bill Buckingham and his wife, Charlotte, were fuming over a textbook that mentioned monkeys in the context of evolution. Bill invoked Christ on the cross, asked a former board member to name the monkey who was his grandfather, and told a Dover High graduate attending Penn State that he'd lost his values at a university where he was encouraged to study evolution. Charlotte read from Genesis for fifteen minutes, telling board members and teachers this is the only truth and this is all you can teach. Board member Heather Geesey joined Bill Buckingham in a chorus of "amens" to his wife's sermon, then said that any teacher who talked to a lawyer should be fired. Spectators in the packed room shouted. One teacher raced to the mike and challenged Geesey.

Yet a few weeks after the June board meeting, something miraculous happened in Dover. The textbook standoff was resolved, the board's feelings calmed, a compromise made possible, and critics of the biology text disarmed.

All because of a public policy decision made in Texas.

Texas and California are the two largest single-adoption textbook markets in the country, where texts are adopted statewide rather than by individual school districts. California is known for its occasional flirtation with bad public policy. In Texas we've been wedded to it for decades. On church and state issues, for almost a century. It was Governor Ma Ferguson who settled a dispute about foreign language teaching in public schools by pointing to her King James Bible and saying, "If English was good enough for Jesus Christ, it's good enough for the schoolchildren of Texas." Much of our worst policy is made by the popularly elected Texas State Board of Education, which seems to honor Governor Ferguson every time it meets. Christian censors, vigilante patriots, flat-earthers, and Holocaust deniers all know there is no better forum for textbook editing than the Texas state board. Publishers genuflect before TSBOE board members, rewriting entire textbooks to accommodate them. And because it's too costly to print separate versions, textbooks vetted and edited in Texas are the textbooks sold to public schools in the other forty-nine states.

An example of why you don't want our state deciding your child's textbook content is the Great State's recent "Battle of the Bulge." The call to arms in 2002 came from a social studies teacher reviewing a sample copy of an eighth-grade textbook. She was bothered by a bulge between General Washington's legs, as depicted in Emanuel Leutze's *Washington Crossing the Delaware.* The vigilant teacher looked at review copies sent by two other publishers, found the same painting and the same bothersome bulge. She began to worry that eighth graders looking at the nineteenth-century masterpiece might conclude that the nation's founding father had a penis. (Perhaps he did, but the bulge in Leutze's painting is a watch fob.)

Publishers responded by electronically emasculating our Founding Father. McGraw-Hill, for example, darkened the area around Washington's crotch. Holt substituted a bulge-free knockoff of the same painting by a Leutze understudy. Only in Prentice Hall's *The American Nation* does *George Washington Crossing the Delaware* appear exactly as he hangs in the Metropolitan Museum of Art in New York.

It was Dover's good fortune that Prentice Hall wasn't so resolute in its defense of Miller and Levine's 2004 edition of *Biology*. Responding to the Texas board, in the book's new edition the publisher had already softened its content—predictably, regarding Darwin's diabolical theory of evolution. For the beleaguered science faculty at Dover High School, the Texas dumb-down of *Biology* was a godsend. Dover's curriculum committee reviewed the new edition and realized that the publisher had produced a book that would pass Bill Buckingham's religious test.

They were mistaken.

Bill Buckingham had already found a textbook that replaces Darwin's process of natural selection with an intelligent designer most readers will recognize as God. *Of Pandas and People* is published by the Foundation for Thought and Ethics, based in Fort Worth, Texas. The FTE was founded in 1983 to promote the teaching of creationism. A lawyer from the Thomas More Law Center steered Buckingham toward *Pandas* and assured him that Thomas More would defend Dover schools pro bono if anyone sued. He suggested that "intelligent design" was a better choice of words than "creationism"—and put Buckingham in touch with the Discovery Institute in Seattle, where intelligent design is packaged, wrapped, and sold to school districts across the country.

The Thomas More Law Center, named in honor of the pious chancellor of England beheaded by Henry VIII in 1535 and canonized by the Roman Catholic Church in 1935, is not your father's law firm. Founded by Domino's Pizza magnate Tom Monaghan, who also founded Ave Maria University and Ave Maria School of Law in Michigan, the TMLC takes the extreme Christian right's cultural wars to the courthouse. Tom Monaghan isn't a typical Christian philanthropist. He is considering, for example, moving the Ave Maria law school to his planned Ave Maria Town, a religious utopia in Florida. He explains: "You won't be able to buy a *Playboy* or *Hustler* in Ave Maria Town. We're going to control the cable television that comes in the area. There is not going to be any pornographic television in Ave Maria Town. If you go to the drugstore and you want to buy the pill or the condoms or contraception, you won't be able to get that in Ave Maria Town."

The Discovery Institute promotes intelligent design and other right-wing favorites, such as bioethics (opposition to stem cell research and physician-assisted suicide) and climate science (opposition to methods to curb global warming). Thomas More defends the principles of Christian faith in court. Once Bill Buckingham teamed up with Tom Monaghan's lawyers and the Discovery Institute, history was about to happen in Dover. Buckingham rounded up enough board votes to block the adoption of *Biology* unless *Pandas* was adopted as a companion text. He wasn't concerned that the small, financially strapped school district didn't have the funds to purchase both textbooks. He was holding the secular biology (there's a concept) text hostage.

Angie Yingling moved the board back into equilibrium. Torn between a commitment of support she'd made to Buckingham and the interests of the schoolchildren she was elected to serve, Yingling changed her vote and joined the four board members who had moved to approve Prentice Hall's *Biology* at an August 2004 board meeting.

She said she wanted to help Buckingham out: "He wants kids to understand that you might not be descended from apes, you know, something against Darwin's theory." But she didn't want to be responsible for biology students starting the next school year without textbooks.

"How could you be so stupid!" Buckingham screamed at her after the meeting. He then impugned the faith of board members, including Alan Bonsell. Miller and Levine's *Biology* was approved and would be delivered just before students arrived in September 2004.

Bill Buckingham then turned his attention to curriculum.

By October 2004, he and Bonsell were ready to vote on a four-paragraph antievolution disclaimer. They knew the new policy might well result in a lawsuit. But Buckingham had told his colleagues on the board he was ready to go to court. Intelligent design was a wedge and Dover a local front in a national campaign to change the law of the land—so that someday American kids would again read the Bible and pray in school. Buckingham wanted to take the new biology curriculum to court. To the U.S. Supreme Court if necessary. A lawsuit would be an opportunity to confront the "liberals in black robes." Buckingham, in fact, was part of a national movement advanced by Discovery Institute propagandists and Thomas More litigators and supported by thousands of Christian-right congregations that George Bush recognized as the Republican Party's base.

To protect Christian students in Dover, before evolution was discussed in biology class, teachers would read a brief statement:

> The Pennsylvania Academic Standards require students to learn about Darwin's Theory of Evolution and eventually to take a standardized test of which evolution is a part.
>
> Because Darwin's Theory is a theory, it continues to be tested as new evidence is discovered. The Theory is not a fact. Gaps in the theory exist for which there is not evidence. A theory is defined as a well-tested explanation that unifies a broad range of observations.

> Intelligent Design is an explanation of the origins of life that differs from Darwin's view. The reference book *Of Pandas and People* is available in the library with other resources for students who might be interested in gaining an understanding of what Intelligent Design actually involves.
>
> With respect to any theory, students are required to keep an open mind. The school leaves the discussion of the Origins of Life to individual students and their families. As a Standards-driven district, class instruction focuses on preparing students to achieve proficiency on Standards-based assessments.

As the board prepared to vote on the statement, Science Department chair Bert Spahr stood up and read from a typed page. It was unlike anything she had done during her forty years teaching in the Dover schools. She told board members they were placing two "of my young untenured teachers" in an impossible position. State standards required science teachers to teach evolution. The board was requiring them to make a statement about intelligent design that would undermine the evolution content mandated by the state.

Spahr pleaded with the board to reconsider:

> The science department, including all of its members, vehemently oppose the board curriculum committee's draft that includes the words intelligent design in our curriculum. It has been deemed unlawful, illegal, and unconstitutional to teach intelligent design, which we thought was a synonym for creationism and/or creation science, along with evolution. . . .
>
> The inclusion will open the district and possibly its teachers to lawsuits which we feel will be a blatant misuse of the taxpayers' dollars. We further feel that our many years of professional training and science education has not been considered and [it] appears Mr. Buckingham is only concerned with his own personal agenda. . . .

> Mr. Buckingham, are you going to direct my teachers to teach intelligent design if it appears on the written curriculum?

Spahr mentioned the 1987 U.S. Supreme Court decision that held the teaching of creationism in violation of the Establishment Clause in the First Amendment.

Buckingham stopped her. "Where," he asked, "did you get your law degree?"

Bertha Spahr is a pillar of education in the small community, one of those public school teachers who are an institution within an institution. After an entire career teaching chemistry, she had taught or known almost everyone who graduated from Dover High School. Buckingham treated her as if she were beneath contempt.

His conduct, followed by the five to four vote requiring the reading of an evolution disclaimer, opened up a religious schism unlike anything this small Pennsylvania town had ever seen. Three board members resigned. Angie Yingling said the pressure became too much to bear. Driving to work, she was stopped by a man who stood in front of her car, arms folded, staring at her and challenging her vote against the *Pandas* text. Carol "Casey" Brown, a member of the Curriculum Committee who had read and critiqued every page of every sample text, resigned after Buckingham told her she would burn in hell because she is an Episcopalian. Her husband, Jeff, who admitted he had consulted God before voting on the disclaimer, also resigned. Their departure strengthened the evangelicals' grip on the board, as they appointed interim members who supported their views.

On the Friday before the evolution disclaimer was to be read to students, the biology teachers refused to distribute the written notice informing parents their children could opt out of the reading of the disclaimer. The teachers also advised the board that they would not read the disclaimer. Biology teacher Jennifer Miller, the daughter of a Church of Christ minister, explained why:

> By reading the statement to our students it essentially was—it was going to be very contradictory to the students by saying, number one, that intelligent design is science, which we didn't believe it was, and that would be misrepresenting the subject matter.
>
> And number two, if I'm telling the students that I'm going to teach evolution, which is very important and they are going to be tested on it, but yet ask them to go and read *Of Pandas and People*, which says that evolution didn't occur, to me that's confusing for the students. . . . For them to be tested on evolution but yet say evolution didn't occur confused our students and would misrepresent how important evolutionary theory is to the students.

Citing their ethical obligation to teach the truth, and Section 235.10 of the Pennsylvania Teaching Act, which "provides that the professional educator may not knowingly and intentionally misrepresent subject matter or curriculum," the science faculty at Dover High, men and women of genuine courage, told their board and their superintendent to shove it.

So Superintendent Rich Nilsen and his deputy, Mike Baksa, stood before Dover High's biology classes and read the four-paragraph statement. And a small group of parents began talking about going to court.

> *Bonsell not only wanted prayer in schools and creationism taught in science class, he also wanted to inject religion into the social studies curriculum, as evidenced by his statement to Baksa that he wanted students to learn more about the Founding Fathers and providing Baksa with a book entitled* Myth of Separation *by David Barton.*
>
> —Judge John E. Jones III

Dover's science teachers were first on the front line to defend the separation of church and state. "We were watching the situation in the media," said Pennsylvania's ACLU legal director,

Witold Walczak. "Then we began to hear from teachers in Dover." Teachers were followed by parents, who contacted the ACLU because they were concerned about the *Pandas* text, the religious subtext in the evolution disclaimer, and the overt religious nature of board meetings.

Tammy Kitzmiller, the mother of an independent-minded daughter, would be the name plaintiff in a challenge to the board policy. Once a group of parents said they were ready to participate in a lawsuit, Walczak called Eric Rothschild in Philadelphia and asked him to serve as a cooperating attorney. Suddenly, eleven parents in Dover had the backing of Pepper Hamilton, a 450-lawyer firm with an international reach. Rothschild would be assisted by co-counsel from the ACLU and Americans United for Separation of Church and State.

Bill Buckingham was finally getting the lawsuit he wanted.

To write that the faith-based litigators from Thomas More were outmatched is to again demonstrate our grasp of the obvious. The plaintiffs' team usually had more paralegals in court than Thomas More had attorneys. But that's just being outnumbered, a separate issue. The quality of counsel probably had something to do with Darwin's natural selection process, by which the best and the brightest rise to the top. In his late thirties, Pepper Hamilton partner Eric Rothschild had a client list that included the American Nuclear Insurers in a Three Mile Island nuclear plant case; the Commonwealth of Pennsylvania in a $22.5 million insurance case; and an American computer vendor sued for fraud by a bank in the Czech Republic. Rothschild, whose direct and cross-examination of witnesses was a mix of relentlessness and good cheer, was representative of the team of lawyers he led into Judge Jones's courtroom.

The lawyers from Thomas More were men out of time. The last time their side had prevailed in a big evolution lawsuit, William Jennings Bryan was sitting in with the prosecution. They are devout Christian men dedicated to the fight against abortion, gay rights, stem cell research, the teaching of evolution, and the separation of church and state. They also go to court to defend the installation of Ten Commandments monuments on government property and the right to pray silently in school. Their narrow range of experience ensured that they would be outmatched by Rothschild and his team. They were also outmatched because they just weren't as smart as the lawyers representing the plaintiffs. (If you're an insurance underwriter about to lose $20 million, you don't call the Thomas More Law Center.)

The "not smart" factor was evident before the case went to trial. The ACLU had only intended to ask for an injunction to stop the antievolution policy. Then Buckingham, Bonsell, Nilsen, and board member Sheila Harkins met with the lawyers from Thomas More. On the following day, in depositions, all four defendants told the same story, one that omitted all the overt religious comments heard by hundreds of others and reported in the local media.

"They met with [Thomas More Law Center director Richard] Thompson, . . . on the evening of January 2, and on January 3 they all came in with a unique story that defied the historical record," said Walczak. (Have you ever heard a lawyer so elegantly say "the defendants are a bunch of liars"?) "They created a dispute of material fact, which laid the groundwork for a megatrial."

Once it was evident that the evangelicals on the Dover school board were lying and collaborating to hide their religious motivation, the ACLU could more easily put the concept of intelligent design on trial.

The defendants were their own worst enemies (unless that distinction belongs to their lawyers). Since they had denied their religious comments, they couldn't defend and explain them in court. "It was an open field for us to run through," said Rothschild. The plaintiffs' lawyers were free to explain the religious motives of the defendants, then prove that intelligent design was religion masquerading as science. Once Judge Jones admitted ACLU witnesses from the fields of molecular biology, paleontology, philosophy of science, and theology, it was evident that something far larger than a policy decision made by a school board was on trial in Harrisburg, Pennsylvania.

> *I'm a taxpayer in Dover. I'm a citizen of Dover. I'm a citizen of this country. This is just thinly veiled religion. . . . If you were to substitute where it says "intelligent design" the word "creationism" there would be no question that this would be a violation of the First Amendment. I've come to accept the fact that we're in the minority view on this. You know, I've read the polls. . . . A lot of people think that it doesn't cross the line. There are a lot of people that don't care. But I care. It crosses my line. . . . There have been letters written about the plaintiffs. We've been called atheists, but we're not. I don't think it matters to the Court, but we're not. We're said to be intolerant of other views. Well, what am I supposed to tolerate? A small encroachment on my First Amendment rights? Well, I'm not going to. I think this is clear what these people have done. And it outrages me.*
> —from the testimony of Dover High School parent FRED CALLAHAN

If they had paid attention to the Establishment Clause James Madison had written for them two hundred years earlier, the evangelical Christians on Dover's school board might have avoided their day in court and the quiet moral authority of Fred Callahan and ten other plaintiffs. But Buckingham, Bonsell, and their lead counsel from Thomas More consider the separation of church and state "a myth."

They didn't buy it.

They should have.

The fight over the biology curriculum and the lawsuit that followed took a terrible toll on this small Pennsylvania community. It was particularly hard on the evangelical Christian board members who decided to mix religion and public policy. Once they cut themselves loose from the moorings the Constitution provides, they seemed to lose sight of their Christian values. The first casualty was the Ninth Commandment—the one that prohibits bearing "false witness against your neighbor." The defendants knew they could prevail only if they could prove that their policy decisions were not influenced by their religious beliefs.

That was a problem.

Journalists who covered the board meetings where the biology curriculum and textbooks were discussed had published accounts of board members openly advocating "creationism." Several quotes by Buckingham suggested a clear religious motivation. Two local papers reported that, at a 2004 board meeting, Buckingham said: "Two thousand years ago someone died on a cross. Can't someone take a stand for him?" The two local newspapers also reported that Buckingham said at one board meeting: "This country wasn't founded on Muslim beliefs or evolution. This country was founded on Christianity, and our students should be taught as such."

If members of the school board openly discussed the religious beliefs that shaped their policy, they were in violation of Supreme Court guidelines that require that public policy (1) must have a secular legislative purpose, (2) can neither advance nor inhibit religion, and (3) must not encourage excessive government entanglement with religion.

The board members settled on a straightforward litigation strategy. They would impugn the integrity of two local reporters.

The board members claimed the reporters "lied," "misquoted," and "made up" their reports. They allowed that Bill Buckingham might have said, "Two thousand years ago someone died on a cross." But if he said it, he said it in November 2003, when the board debated filing an amicus brief in a Supreme Court case regarding the phrase "under God" in the Pledge of Allegiance. Yet no news outlet reported Buckingham's "died on the cross" quote in November 2003, and at least two reported it immediately after the June 14, 2004, board meeting.

The attorneys from Thomas More subpoenaed the two reporters whose published accounts of school board meetings included religious comments by Buckingham, Bonsell, and others on the board. They planned to question the reporters about their political affiliations, religious beliefs, and professional histories, apparently to establish a bias against Buckingham.

Print journalists make mistakes in reporting. But as the title of Dan Rather's autobiography reminds us, "the camera never blinks." Not even the Fox News camera. A June 14, 2004, Fox TV news clip on which Bill Buckingham discusses creationism made the defendants' story hard to believe. As did the fact that *only* the evangelical Christians on the board failed to hear religious comments.

The two reporters refused to sit for such broad-ranging depositions and instead prepared to go to jail. Perhaps because testimony of a dozen other fact witnesses supported the accounts of the subpoenaed reporters, the judge worked out an agreement that kept them out of jail. The defendants and their attorneys from Thomas More had seemed unconcerned that one of the reporters they threatened to send to jail was a mother nursing a four-month-old baby.

It was not Christianity's finest moment.

> *The effect of Defendants' actions in adopting the curriculum change was to impose a religious view of biological origins into the biology course.*
>
> —JUDGE JOHN E. JONES III

Federal district judge John E. Jones III isn't one of the "liberals in black robes" Bill Buckingham believes is eroding the nation's moral foundation. Jones had worked on Pennsylvania governor Tom Ridge's campaign and transition team in 1994 and was appointed to chair the state liquor commission. In his seven years as a commissioner, Jones was best known for banning the sale of Bad Frog Beer—not because of alcoholic content but because the frog on the label, as Amy Worden wrote in *The Philadelphia Inquirer,* was "flipping the bird." (A wise usage, as a frog has no middle finger.) George W. Bush appointed Jones to the federal bench in 2002, a year after he named Ridge secretary of homeland security. The only Bill of Rights case on Jones's docket before the Dover suit involved College Republicans from Shippensburg University who claimed their First Amendment rights were violated by an administration that stopped them from hanging anti–Osama bin Laden posters on campus. Jones ruled that the university violated the students' constitutional right to free speech. The attorney representing the students described the judge as "meticulously prepared" and "mindful of precedent." When the Dover case ended up on Jones's docket, Tom Ridge said the judge was perfectly suited to decide it: "He has an inquisitive mind, a penetrating intellect, and an incredible sense of humor."

With an intense, interested, and sometimes bemused look on his face, Jones presided over a year of pretrial hearings and twenty-one days of testimony, objections, hairsplitting arguments, and attorneys' sidebars. It's what judges are supposed to do, and here is one instance where it's evident that G. W. Bush got it right.

A Paramount movie scout at the trial was hoping Tom Hanks would portray Jones in the movie. Hanks will have to turn his genial Everyman sincerity into quiet (and occasionally good-humored) gravitas. The simple dispute between the Dover school board and parents who objected to the religious turn the board was taking could have been settled in state district court. Judge Jones decided to address something much larger. Since that 1987 Supreme Court decision ruled the teaching of "creation science" a violation of the Establishment Clause, fundamentalist Christian extremists have looked for a Trojan horse to introduce their biblical version of the origin of life into the nation's science classes.

"Intelligent design" was that Trojan horse. The judge decided to meet it head-on.

There is broad, deep, and well-financed institutional support for reintroducing religion into the public schools, and the Discovery Institute is a big institutional player. The institute markets itself as a think tank focused on the teaching of science and free-market economics and never mentions religion. It's been unmasked as a pack of religious antimoderns who would just as soon see the current pope take another whack at Galileo. Discovery's "Wedge Strategy" document, leaked to the public in 1999, begins with a statement about the erosion of the "bedrock principle . . . that man is created in the image of God" and lays out a program to replace "materialistic explanations with the theistic understanding that nature and human beings are created by God." Founded by former Reagan White House official Bruce Chapman, Discovery got $1.5 million in startup funding from Howard Ahmanson. Ahmanson, heir to a California savings and loan fortune, also invested in Christian Reconstructionist groups advancing the teachings of the late Rousas J. Rushdoony, whose theology is so toxic that even the most batshit American evangelicals disavow him. (The execution of adulterers, homosexuals, witches, and incorrigible children can be a hard sell.)

At times it seemed as if all the country's religious whack jobs were on the school board Rolodex in Dover. The WallBuilders is an advocacy ministry founded by David Barton, the former vice chair of the Texas Republican Party who was hired by the Republican National Committee to work the Christian base in the 2004 elections. The WallBuilders' campaign to return God to his central place in social studies and American history curricula was the next big thing coming to Dover. Once he got his intelligent design curriculum in place, Alan Bonsell intended to use WallBuilders texts and programs to fix Dover's social studies curriculum.

Discovery, Thomas More, and the WallBuilders are part of a broad national movement determined to return the country to its theocentric roots. All are connected to the Republican Party at the state and national levels. All have ties to Republican congressional leaders. And all have strong financial backing.

Yet eleven parents, a few teachers, the ACLU, and Americans United for Separation of Church and State stood squarely in their way.

Judge Jones could have ruled that the Dover school board violated the Establishment Clause and stopped there. He went far beyond that, ruling that intelligent design is not science but "an untestable alternative hypothesis grounded in religion [and thrust] into the science classroom to misrepresent well-established propositions." It is, therefore, "unconstitutional to teach ID as an alternative to evolution in public school classrooms."

In a thorough and sometimes angry opinion, the judge referred to the blatantly dishonest editing of *Of Pandas and People*, which occurred immediately after the Supreme Court banned teaching creationism in public schools. "Cognates of the word creation (creationism and creationist), which appeared approximately 150 times were deliberately and systemically replaced with the phrase *ID*." Jones cited the five-year plan in the Discovery Institute's wedge document, whose goal it is to "replace science as currently practiced with a 'theistic and Christian science.' " He observed that fundamentalist organizations were formed precisely to promote the idea that the "Book of Genesis was supported by scientific data." He documented the "long history of Fundamentalism's attack on the scientific theory of evolution." And he quoted one of the plaintiffs' expert witnesses who testified that to teach students that intelligent design is science is to "make them stupid."

Closer to home, Judge Jones excoriated the Christian activists on the school board who for hidden religious purposes had divided their community and violated the separation clause in the First Amendment. "The citizens of Dover were poorly served by the members of the Board who voted for the ID policy. It is ironic that several of these individuals, who so staunchly and proudly touted their religious convictions in public, would time and again lie to cover their tracks and disguise the real purpose behind the ID Policy."

Jones also quoted the "poignant speech" that Carol Brown made when she resigned from the board:

> There has been a slow but steady marginalization of some board members. Our opinions are no longer valued or listened to. Our contributions have been minimized or not acknowledged at all. A measure of that is the fact that I myself have been twice asked within the past year if I was "born again." No one has, nor should have the right, to ask that of a fellow board member. An individual's religious beliefs should have no impact on his or her ability to serve as a school board director, nor should a person's beliefs be used as a yardstick to measure the value of that service. However, it has become increasingly evident that it is the direction the board has now chosen to go, holding a certain religious belief is of paramount importance.

The judge also incorporated into his opinion a short passage from the resignation speech of board member Noel Weinrich: "I was referred to as unpatriotic, and my religious beliefs were questioned. I served in the U.S. Army for eleven years and six years on the board. Seventeen years of my life have been devoted to public service, and my religion is personal. It's between me, God, and my pastor."

Judge Jones's 139-page opinion, said ACLU lawyer Walczak, "is a playbook for any citizen fighting intelligent design in a public school classroom." It is binding only on the Middle District of

Pennsylvania, but its judicial craftsmanship and methodical application of precedent make it a road map for any federal judge adjudicating religion in the public schools.

Few school board members across the country will want to see themselves described as Judge Jones described the extremist majority that controlled the Dover board:

> Those who disagree with our holding will likely mark it as the product of an activist judge. If so, they will have erred as this is manifestly not an activist Court. Rather, this case came to us as the result of the activism of an ill-informed faction on a school board, aided by a national public interest law firm eager to find a constitutional test case on ID, who in combination drove the Board to adopt an imprudent and ultimately unconstitutional policy. The breathtaking inanity of the Board's decision is evident when considered against the factual backdrop which has now been fully revealed through this trial. The students, parents, and teachers of the Dover Area School District deserved better than to be dragged into this legal maelstrom, with its resulting utter waste of monetary and personal resources.

There were financial consequences. Before filing suit, Eric Rothschild wrote a letter to the board, warning them of substantial legal fees if the plaintiffs prevailed. The tab for the lawsuit exceeded $3 million. Plaintiffs' attorneys waived all but $1 million, the total out-of-pocket expenses, such as hotels, airfare, photocopying, and stenography, incurred in the yearlong process—and offered the district a discount for early payoff. They asked Judge Jones to enter $2 million in legal fees into the public record, so other school districts considering intelligent design policy would be aware of the consequences.

"Pennsatucky" is the regional pejorative that snooty cultural cartographers use to point the way to Dogpatch, Pennsylvania. Dover ain't exactly Dogpatch, but it's a hundred miles and a hundred years from Philadelphia. It's the northern extension of Appalachia, 98 percent white, 70 percent Republican, devoutly religious, and predominantly Protestant. Everyone, it seems, goes to church. It is as unlikely a place as any in the country for such a resounding court victory vindicating the First Amendment.

After plaintiff and parent Fred Callahan concluded his breathtaking courtroom soliloquy, asking, "What am I supposed to tolerate? A small encroachment on my First Amendment rights? Well, I'm not going to," an absolute hush fell over the courtroom. In the jury box, where the press was seated, the silence was broken by a British reporter who leaned toward his American colleagues and said sotto voce:

"You know, I think the people we're looking at here are the very best of your country."

POSTSCRIPT

Dover finally had enough of Alan Bonsell and Bill Buckingham imposing their beliefs on the faculty and students. A week after the trial concluded, and a month before Judge Jones handed down his decision, voters swept all eight incumbents out of office, replacing them with a reform slate opposed to the intelligent design curriculum. The two most vocal advocates of the ID policy got the fewest votes. Superintendent Nilsen's contract for the following school year was not renewed.

Televangelist Pat Robertson warned of the loss of God's grace. Ten years earlier he'd threatened Orlando with "earthquakes, tornadoes, and possibly a meteor" after a gay day at Disney World, but nothing materialized. He hedged his bets on Dover: "I'd just like to say to the good citizens of Dover, if there is a disaster in your area, don't turn to God. You just rejected Him from your city. And don't wonder why He hasn't helped you when problems begin, if they begin. I'm not saying they will, but if they do, just remember, you just voted God out of your city."

Since Judge Jones ruled in the Kitzmiller case, no school board in the nation has succeeded in adopting an intelligent design biology curriculum. In fact, they are backing away from unconstitutional policy. A year after *Kitzmiller* was decided, the Cobb County, Georgia, school board settled with a group of parents in the district, agreeing to remove antievolution warning stickers from biology textbooks. They also agreed, in negotiations with Americans United for Separation of Church and State and attorney Eric Rothschild, to refrain from any and all acts of interference with the teaching of evolution in biology classes.

FIVE

Sneaking and Peeking

The right of the people to be secure in their persons, houses, papers, and effects, against unreasonable searches and seizures, shall not be violated, and no Warrants shall issue, but upon probable cause, supported by Oath or affirmation, and particularly describing the place to be searched, and the persons or things to be seized.

—Fourth Amendment to the United States Constitution

There can be no doubt that behind all the actions of this court of justice, that is to say in my case, behind my arrest and today's interrogation, there is a great organization at work. An organization which not only employs corrupt warders, oafish Inspectors, and Examining Magistrates. . . . And the significance of this great organization, gentlemen? It consists in this, that innocent persons are accused of guilt, and senseless proceedings are put in motion against them.

—Franz Kafka, *The Trial*

You can't trade your freedom for security. Because in the end you lose both.

—Brandon Mayfield, *The Oregonian*

Hanging on the wall of Brandon Mayfield's law office in a small suburban Portland, Oregon, strip mall is a framed copy of the Bill of Rights. It's not something Mayfield consults when dealing with the wills, custody disputes, and immigration work that pay the bills for his family of five. And it seems out of place among the degrees, diplomas, and certificates also hanging on the wall. Mayfield himself seems out of place when he appears in court. A slight, boyish thirty-eight, with short red hair and a trim beard that might be intended to add gravitas, Mayfield looks more like a law student than a lawyer.

You can't spend too much time with Brandon Mayfield without recognizing that his values are midwestern American. Native of Kansas, career as a military officer ended by a shoulder injury, shingle hanging out in Aloha, Oregon, framed copy of the Bill of Rights on the office wall. Clearly more Kansas than Kafka. But a careful reading of Kafka would have been useful in the trial Mayfield was beginning in May 2004. Maybe more useful than the criminal proceedings courses he took in law school. As useful as the ten amendments hanging on his office wall.

A material witness proceeding in federal court is not very common and was new territory for Mayfield. So he was uneasy sitting at the defense table when the bailiff ordered "All rise" and Judge Robert Jones walked into the courtroom.

The proceeding wasn't exactly familiar territory for the judge, either. The first thing he said as he took his seat at the bench was "Just a minute." Federal judges are all about decorum and authority. "Just a minute" is not how most trials get under way.

"Just a minute," Judge Jones repeated. "Who are all these people?"

"In the courtroom are five FBI agents—four agents," said assistant U.S. attorney Pamala Holsinger.

"Are they authorized people?" asked the judge.

"They're all authorized, Your Honor," Holsinger said.

In this country, at least until recently, anyone who walks into a courtroom and sits quietly is "authorized" to be there.

Authorized people was a novel concept for Mayfield. He had limited experience in federal court and wasn't sure where the hearing was headed. He wasn't familiar with the first case the judge cited: *United States v. Awadallah.* But it had been decided only six months earlier, and Judge Jones told the clerk to get Mayfield a copy. "Since you're a lawyer," the judge said, "I think it's a good thing that you read this case."

Maybe Tom Nelson, the older attorney sitting next to Mayfield at the defense counsel table, had read *Awadallah.* At least Mayfield could follow the courtroom routine as the judge began plodding through the standard procedural steps—asking about the search warrant, asking if the proper warrants were left in the seized vehicles, asking if the house and office searched were left in order. "We don't want to have some claim of some drawer [*sic*] was pulled out and left all over the floor and that sort of thing."

Mayfield felt a little better when the judge praised his service to his country "as an enlisted man and an officer." But he was still nervous and uncomfortable in the blue suit he had never before worn to court.

When it was finally his turn to address the judge, Brandon Bieri Mayfield adjusted his leg irons and gave it his best shot. "That's not my fingerprint, Your Honor," he said. At the moment, he assumed the truth was the best defense and might even set him free.

Here's why a reading of Kafka might have been useful: Brandon Mayfield wasn't charged with a crime. He wasn't a criminal defendant. Yet according to what the judge was telling him, he could be detained indefinitely. That was what *Awadallah* touched on—along with prosecution for perjury should a material witness perjure himself, intentionally or unintentionally.

Mayfield might be released if he would testify under oath about the crime. But he knew nothing about the crime. Then again, even if he agreed to a deposition or testimony before a grand jury, he might not be released. He was caught in a judicial web similar to the one that had ensnared the protagonist of Kafka's novel. Mayfield didn't know the charges against him, yet his freedom depended on what he said. He could be held indefinitely if he didn't talk.

"These proceedings are closed; that is, they are secret," the judge said. A locked-down court. No unauthorized persons. No press. No public witnesses to the hearings. Halls and elevators cleared when Mayfield was shuttled from the Multnomah County detention center over to the courtroom in the modern Mark O. Hatfield Justice Center in downtown Portland. As the case got under way, Mayfield was even provided a pseudonym.

There was also the issue of the death penalty. The crime the FBI agents and U.S. attorneys were trying to pin on Mayfield was punishable by death. Even if he wasn't yet charged, Brandon Mayfield knew that he could be facing execution. As did Tom Nelson. A proper defense for the crime federal prosecutors were investigating could cost as much as a million dollars and put all of Nelson's other clients on hold. And Nelson wasn't a criminal defense lawyer. Yet he couldn't let a friend walk into a federal court and represent himself when he possibly faced execution.

Let us digress to remind readers that both authors are from Texas, where executions are so routine that, by holding office for six years, Governor George W. Bush set records you have to travel to China or Iran to match. Yet not even in Texas do we conduct closed trials when a person's life is in play. And we avoid holding a man as a witness against himself.

Brandon Mayfield had been surprised when two FBI agents walked into his office on a May morning in 2004. There had been some warning, even if he and his wife, Mona, had misread it. While Mona and Brandon Mayfield were working at the law office, and the three kids were at school, odd things were happening in their house. They found blinds readjusted at the end of the day. Dead bolts the Mayfields never locked were locked when the family returned home in the evening. Footprints of odd shoes were all over the carpets, though the Mayfields don't wear shoes in their house. Even school papers the children left at home were disturbed.

Brandon Mayfield called the local police, who turned up nothing. But the FBI was the last thing on his mind. There was no reason for anyone to investigate him. Yet federal agents had been in his house for weeks, planting wiretaps, downloading computer files, taking hundreds of photos. If the local police knew, they couldn't share what they knew with Mayfield.

The sneak-and-peek provisions of the USA Patriot Act allow secret, delayed notification warrants to search homes, offices, and electronic files. FBI agents had been working the Mayfield home, even if they forgot that the sneak-and-peek provisions of the Patriot Act require agents to be sneaky. Mayfield still didn't get it when the two agents walked into his office and told him they had some questions to ask him.

"If you have questions, put them in writing. I'll review them and might get back to you," he told the agents. Then he was frisked and handcuffed. At his first appearance in court, he told Judge Jones that the officers were kind enough (he vaguely knew one of them) to cuff his hands in front so the handcuffs wouldn't be so visible when he walked out of his office. He told the two agents that if he were seen walking out of his office in handcuffs, his law practice would be destroyed. This story is going to get out, one agent said as he eased Mayfield into the Ford Explorer.

"The media is right behind us."

"Brandon, think long and hard," the man playing the bad cop

said once they were in the Explorer. "You remember how the Muslim brothers stood up for Mike Hawash? Well, they are not going to be there for you." Maher "Mike" Hawash was one of the Portland Seven, a hapless group of local jihadists who set out to join the Taliban, never made it to Afghanistan, yet all ended up serving long terms in federal prison.

Two months before Mayfield was picked up, a series of bombs on commuter trains in Madrid had killed two hundred people and injured two thousand more. The Spanish National Police had found latent fingerprints on a bag the terrorists had left behind. One of them was analyzed by the feds and determined to be Brandon Mayfield's right index fingerprint, which had been on file since he was commissioned as an officer in the Army. The agency's forensic lab at Quantico, Virginia, reported that three fingerprint specialists had examined the print and reached the same conclusion.

To support their single-digit theory, veteran FBI agent Richard Werder built a circumstantial case against Mayfield that focused on the Portland Seven.

"Jeffrey Battle along with other co-conspirators, Patrice Lumumba Ford, Ahmed Bilal, Muhammad Bilal, Habis Al Saoub, and Maher Hawash after September 11, 2001, tried but failed to travel to Afghanistan to fight for Al-Quaida [*sic*] and the Taliban against U.S. Forces in the region," wrote Agent Werder in the affidavit the agency used to justify breaking into Mayfield's home and law office.

Battle and others, according to the affidavit, "attempted to get into Afghanistan through Pakistan in order to martyr themselves on the battlefield of Afghanistan. The group made it as far as western China and were unable to reach Afghanistan because they were unable to obtain visas to enter Pakistan." Battle was the most rhetorically over-the-top of the Portland Seven and referred to Americans as "kaffirs," or nonbelievers. Mayfield had once represented Battle in a child custody suit. So Mayfield's role in Battle's child custody case linked him to a group that might have been linked to the terror cells in Spain—even if anyone watching the prosecution of Portland's hapless jihadists would quickly conclude that al-Qaeda they were not. And they had traveled to China, not Spain.

Reading Agent Werder's affidavit would take your breath away if the guy weren't so plodding in plodding to his preordained conclusion.

Werder addresses Mayfield's travel: "The investigation has thus far revealed no record of travel in the United States in the name of Brandon Bieri Mayfield. Checks through the National Tracking System going back one year don't turn up any airline travel or border crossings by Brandon Mayfield. State Department records indicated Mayfield's passport expired October 20, 2003, and he is not on record for renewal. To date, the FBI had not identified any aliases used by Mayfield."

That was Point 22 of the affidavit. In Point 29, Agent Werder digs deeper and finds what "may be relevant evidence of contacts between Mayfield and associates that may have traveled to Madrid, Spain." What follows requires careful reading because the logic is so nuanced: "Since no record or travel documents have been found in the name of Brandon Bieri Mayfield, it is believed Mayfield may have traveled under a false or fictitious name, with false or fictitious documents. It is also believed that if Mayfield did not travel to Spain utilizing false identification documents, that he associated with someone that played a role in the March 11, 2004, terrorist act in Spain."

How could any federal judge resist such an argument?

Agent Werder used the powerful investigative arm of the FBI to establish that Brandon Mayfield had not traveled abroad. Then he explained how the absence of any record of foreign travel might in fact be proof of foreign travel. Then he closed the final loophole to secure his request to search Mayfield's home, office, bank accounts, client files, storage facilities, home and office computer files, safe-deposit boxes, and family cars. And to seize all of his files. Having proved that Mayfield had not traveled abroad but then explained how he probably did, Agent Werder concluded that none of this mattered: "If Mayfield did not travel to Spain utilizing false identification documents, it is believed that he associated with someone that played a role in the March 11, 2004 bombing." The FBI had no idea who that "someone that played a role" was, Werder admitted in the following sentence.

"A real peach" is how Tom Nelson described Werder's affidavit.

"A hodgepodge of irrelevant and unconnected circumstances," according to the federal public defenders who replaced Nelson.

In the political climate after September 11, 2001, practice of the Islamic faith was almost criminalized. The large concentration of Muslims in Portland and across the river in Vancouver, Washington, lived under a cloud of suspicion. By September 2001, Portland already had survived what many of the city's residents considered a close brush with Islamist terrorism. The Algerian "Millennium Bomber" Ahmed Ressam was arrested at the Canadian border just five hours north on I-5—with explosives and a plan to blow up the Los Angeles airport—and federal antiterrorism money flowing into the region heated up the law enforcement climate. Then came sensational front-page accounts in *The Oregonian* of Farid Adlouni's business relationship with Wadih El Hage—"a person identified as the former personal secretary of Usama Bin Laden." Adlouni was charged with nothing but his trial in the press was followed by a spectacular staged and ultimately meaningless arrest of a Muslim cleric in the Portland airport and the overblown trial of the Portland Seven.

Suddenly anyone dressed in anything that deviated from traditional American attire was suspect. Portland being Portland, cross-dressers got a walk. But we can safely observe that by the time FBI agents started digging through the drawers in Brandon and Mona Mayfield's bedroom, bugging his living room, and photocopying Sharia Mayfield's homework, Portland, Oregon, was not a good place for Muslims.

The Mayfields, you see, were Muslim.

The constitutional right that would protect a person, his home, and his property from unreasonable searches and seizures began with John Adams in Massachusetts and was completed by James Madison in Virginia twenty years later. It was the creation of a new right, not the expansion of an existing right. As the constitutional scholar Leonard Levy writes, the Fourth Amendment enshrined in the Constitution the appealing fiction that in England a man's home was his castle. That right barely existed in England. Nor did it exist in England's American colonies: "Reasonable search and seizure approximated whatever the searcher thought reasonable," writes historian William Cuddihy. Colonial customs agents used writs of assistance to seize or tax "uncustomed" goods or to enter homes to inventory liquor, salt, candles, soap, glass, and whatever else was taxable. They dug through barns and root cellars looking for taxable goods, and when they didn't find what they wanted, they put devout believers under oath and asked them what spirits they had consumed over the past year—then taxed them for them. A man's castle was no safer from unreasonable search in colonial America than in Brandon Mayfield's suburban Oregon.

A young John Adams got interested in the topic when he rode into town from Braintree to watch James Otis argue a case in superior court. Open-ended writs that allowed customs agents to enlist local magistrates to search warehouses and homes weren't a big hit in Boston. When authorities in London reauthorized the writs after the death of George II, in 1760, sixty-two Boston merchants rebelled and James Otis took up their case.

James Otis, Jr., belonged to an established Massachusetts family, was ten years older than Adams, had wasted two years at Harvard before getting serious about his studies, graduated after seven years, and spent two more holed up in his family's Barnstable home reading the classics. He was familiar enough with the classics to toss off a line of Virgil: *Flectere si nequeo superos, Acheronta movebo*—"If heaven I cannot bend, then hell I'll stir." In Boston's Town Hall in 1761, Otis was raising hell. He had walked away from his job as advocate general for the Vice Admiralty Courts, gone native, and was pro bono counsel for Boston merchants fighting writs of assistance. "In such a cause, I despise all fees!" Otis said. He turned a fight over tax collection into an eloquent statement of a fundamental principle that didn't yet exist. "A man's house is his castle," Otis said to the judges. "And whilst he is quiet, he is as well guarded as a prince in his castle."

John Adams was a young country lawyer from down the pike in Braintree. "Otis was a flame on Fire!" Adams wrote years later. Flame or not, he lost his case. Yet Adams later wrote that the fight against the writs of assistance was the "commencement of the controversy between Great Britain and America." When Massachusetts included a protection against search and seizure in its state constitution in 1780, James Otis was moving John Adams's hand:

> Every subject has a right to be secure from all unreasonable searches, and seizures, of his person, his houses, his papers, and all his possessions. All warrants, therefore, are contrary to this right, if the cause or foundation of them be not previously supported by oath or affirmation; and if the order in the warrant to a civil officer, to make search in suspected places, to attest one or more suspected persons, or seize their property, be not ac-

> companied with a special designation of the persons or objects of search, arrest, or seizure: and no warrant ought to be issued but in cases, and with the formalities prescribed by the laws.

When James Madison set out to persuade the U.S. Congress to adopt a Bill of Rights, he found the source for his Fourth Amendment in the state constitution of Massachusetts. Madison's draft included broad provisions and substituted a muscular imperative for Adams's wimpy "ought." A House committee deleted "unreasonable searches, and seizures"—the heart of the amendment. Congressman Elbridge Gerry of Massachusetts reinserted the phrase because he thought it had been deleted by mistake.

There was far more to the history of the Fourth Amendment than a fight with tax collectors, even if John Adams latched on to the idea when Boston merchants turned on the king's tax men. Agents of the Crown frequently used searches to suppress political dissent, tossing the offices of political pamphleteers and using their private writings to declare them guilty of sedition. On one occasion during the Revolution, colonial authorities seized the political papers and records of forty of their fellow Pennsylvanians, who were arrested and deported without trial for being disloyal to the American cause. Colonial authorities said the attack on their countrymen was necessary because the country was "at war."

"At war" was the justification the feds used in Oregon—225 years after American colonial authorities in Pennsylvania expelled a bunch of questionable Quakers with no regard for their civil liberties. Like his forebears in Pennsylvania, FBI agent Richard Werder considered himself a foot soldier on the front lines of a war—in this case the Bush administration's War on Terror.

"If the world that is reflected in Richard Werder's affidavit exists, we're really in trouble," said Tom Nelson, who eagerly turned Mayfield's case over to federal public defenders with the resources to put on a proper defense.

We're really in trouble.

Werder's affidavit included more than convoluted logic about Brandon Mayfield's travel. It is a long bill of particulars that lacks the particulars that justified locking up Brandon Mayfield. Brandon Mayfield is married to Mona Mayfield, a.k.a. Mona Mohamed, a naturalized American citizen born in Egypt, according to Werder's affidavit. Mona Mayfield's cell phone was used to place one call to Pete Seda, in Ashland, Oregon. Seda, also known as Perouz Sedaghaty, had been U.S. director of the Al-Haramain Islamic Foundation, a charity "headquartered in Riyadh, Saudi Arabia, with offices throughout the world. Six offices of the AHIF have been designated as specially designated terrorist organizations by the United States Department of the Treasury. . . . This designation did not include the AHIF offices in the United States."

While under surveillance, according to Agent Werder, Mayfield had been seen driving to the Bilal Mosque in Beaverton, Oregon. "On several occasions" each day.

Mayfield's law practice was advertised in the Business Link Directory, owned by Farid Adlouni in Portland. Adlouni had once been in business with Wadih El Hage, the "person identified as the former personal secretary of Usama Bin Laden," convicted in New York of conspiring to murder U.S. nationals and committing perjury regarding the U.S. embassy bombings in Kenya and Tanzania in August 1998. When questioned, Adlouni admitted that Business Link was a "Muslim Yellow Pages."

Much of Werder's affidavit reads like a halal version of Six Degrees of Kevin Bacon. Mayfield is suspect because he associated with individuals who associated with individuals who associated with other individuals.

The FBI was in transition from an agency that solved crimes already committed to an agency that prevented crimes that might happen—a necessity in light of what occurred on September 11,

2001. Yet that transition was a dangerous moment for people of one faith. Take the Werder affidavit and substitute "church." Or "synagogue." Substitute "Christian Business Guide" with the stylized fish on the cover. Or "Jewish Yellow Pages." Substitute "Bible" or "Torah." Substitute "Family Research Council" or "American Israel Public Affairs Committee." Fill in the blanks in the Werder affidavit with Christian or Jewish references in place of Islamic references and the American public would rise up in anger.

Brandon Mayfield went to jail on a religion rap.

Of course, there was the fingerprint. And the FBI.

We're Americans. We read newspapers. We read magazines. Mostly, though, we watch TV. So we know that our Federal Bureau of Inspection has no peers. Isn't the FBI the gold standard in criminal forensic science?

We wonder.

Brandon Mayfield's life was on the line when he was escorted into federal court in Portland. So it's not as if he was an unbiased observer. But in his attempt to defend himself in court, he pointed out some serious flaws in the forensic case the government was building against him.

"We are talking about a fingerprint that was provided by the SP, the Spanish Police," Mayfield said. "That was a photograph of a latent print on this alleged bag. . . . There is a photograph. We don't have a chain of evidence. It's not the [American] federal police that conducted the investigation gathering of this alleged bag. It was provided to somebody here. I read the affidavit. There is some conflict about their matching fingerprint."

Mayfield was scoring on technical points. And, like the rest of us, he assumed the FBI was thorough, competent, and honest. If only the right FBI agents could get a good look at the hard evidence, he believed he would be cleared.

But Mayfield's problem wasn't so much the flawed chain of custody. It was the bad link at the end of the chain, in Quantico. The Spanish National Police found a backpack full of detonators in a van used by the terrorists. They forwarded the prints to the FBI. The boys at Quantico ran the prints through their database and came up with twenty potential matches.

The potential matches, Results 1 through 20, were sent to the Latent Fingerprint Unit at Quantico. Along with the information that Latent Fingerprint 17 belonged to a Muslim. The fingerprint allegedly belonging to Mayfield was the only one with a religious affiliation. These guys must have studied the *Saturday Night Live* police lineup skit that put John Belushi, Tom Schiller, and Chevy Chase in line with Richard Pryor in handcuffs. Mayfield was a Muslim living in a city considered by many, certainly many in the agency, to be the national capital of radical Islamic extremism. Like Richard Pryor, Print 17 stuck out like a sore thumb.

The "Muslim factor" was not the only flaw in the FBI's fingerprint process. Consider. The analysis of the Muslim print from Spain began with a senior FBI examiner who received an image file of Print 17, along with the nineteen other possible hits from the database. He concluded that the Spanish print matched Mayfield's right index finger and forwarded his report to a private consultant who worked as a "verifier." The verifier—a former agent who had been reprimanded at least three times for misidentifying fingerprints while he was at the agency—verified what was sent to him by the senior examiner. But he was verifying the senior examiner's conclusion, not conducting his own analysis of a fresh set of prints.

The conclusion of the two analysts was then sent to the unit supervisor. He knew he was looking at a Muslim fingerprint that had been matched by two examiners. If the FBI was slacking on quality control, they were close enough for government work. Latent Fingerprint 17, through a process lacking in independent evaluation and corrupted by the knowledge that the print had a religious affiliation, was *conclusively* matched with Brandon Mayfield's right index finger.

Mayfield wasn't the only one to get the finger.

Back in Madrid, the Spanish National Police had done their own analysis and reached their own conclusion. Twenty-six days before two FBI agents walked into Brandon Mayfield's law office, cuffed him, and took him to jail, the Spaniards informed the FBI there was "no match." The FBI promptly dispatched an agent (who did not speak Spanish) to Madrid to convince the Spanish National Police that they were wrong. The Spaniards stood by their analysis.

Not to let forensic facts stand in the way of an important investigation, the FBI took its analysis of LFP 17 to a secret Foreign Intelligence Surveillance Act (FISA) court in Washington, D.C., and obtained the secret warrant that got them into the Mayfield home. Then, with bugs planted in the house and big-footed agents stomping the carpets and locking the wrong doors, agents juiced up the language enough to persuade a federal judge to open the doors of Brandon Mayfield's bank account and law office.

According to Agent Werder, the three FBI print analysts considered "LFP #17 a 100% positive identification." The affidavit mentioned that "preliminary findings" of the Spanish police "were not consistent" with the FBI's analysis. In fact, the final conclusions of the Spanish National Police completely contradicted the FBI findings.

Something must have been lost in translation. In the end, Werder wrote, the Spanish police "felt satisfied with the FBI laboratory's investigation." The forensic investigators back at SNP headquarters in Madrid must have been saying: *¡Qué gilipollas!* (What dumbshits!)

And somewhere J. Edgar Hoover must have been turning over in his closet.

If it was Mayfield's misfortune to be a Muslim investigated by the FBI in Portland, at least the city is home to several of the best federal public defenders in the country. "Quality of public defenders varies," said Tom Nelson. "Brandon had excellent representation with Steve Wax." Wax, the senior public defender in the city, has been a criminal defense lawyer for twenty-six years. He is dispassionate, erudite, cautious, and attentive to detail. Sitting in his seventeenth-floor office in front of a huge window overlooking the Willamette River, he described some of the difficulties in representing Brandon Mayfield.

To begin with, Mayfield was not a defendant. But he could make himself one if he said the wrong thing. Wax didn't want his client testifying before a grand jury, because there is no right to counsel when appearing before a grand jury. An innocent mistake, contradicting something you previously said, misstating something, can be construed as perjury. Defense attorneys know that grand juries can be "perjury traps." Asked if he believed Mayfield was innocent, Wax dismissed the question. "Sometimes guilt or innocence is irrelevant in a criminal proceeding," he said. "We wanted to keep [Mayfield] in the material witness box and out of the defendant box."

The material witness statute is an odd duck. Traditionally it has been used to detain one party to preserve his testimony against another party. It was useful in prosecuting mobsters because one member of a crime syndicate could be detained (and protected) until he testified against another. The process was straightforward. Witness A was detained to testify against Subject B. Then Witness A was released—sometimes into the Federal Witness Protection Program (which in Spanish is called *Arizona*).

As a U.S. attorney locking up mobsters in New Jersey, Bush's homeland security czar, Michael Chertoff, had devised a creative use of the material witness statute. He detained suspects and held them as witnesses against themselves. Witness A would be sweated until he testified against Witness A. It's as novel as it is frightening. Attorney General John Ashcroft, who was never too prissy about rights of the accused, loved it. Make a man a witness against himself and watch him squirm until he talks.

Chertoff, who as assistant attorney general was one of the architects of the Patriot Act, believes the government gets a bang for its buck with material witness detentions. "Bear in mind that you get not only testimony," he told a Senate committee. "You get fingerprints, you get hair samples, so there's all kinds of evidence you can get from a witness.

"Are we being aggressive and hard-nosed?" Chertoff said at his confirmation hearing. "You bet. But let me emphasize that every step we have taken satisfies the Constitution and federal law as it existed both before and after September 11."

"We're in a time of war," Chertoff had warned the American Bar Association two years earlier, when he was a federal appellate judge. That war had arrived in Oregon. It was much larger than Brandon Mayfield. In September 2002, eight months before Mayfield was detained, armed agents surrounded Portland's most prominent Muslim cleric. The FBI had flown in its top brass from D.C. and shut down a Portland airport concourse to arrest the leader of the As-Saber Mosque in southwest Portland. They had obtained a warrant for the arrest of Sheikh Mohamed Abdirahman Kariye several days earlier and could have picked him up at home. Instead, they arrested him in the airport as he was leaving the country (which they already knew was his intent). They claimed the popular religious leader had traces of explosives in his luggage and was carrying "a large amount" of money.

Kariye was locked up for five weeks until explosives tests came back a false positive. The thirty thousand dollars he had on him was money for him and his sons to get established in the United Arab Emirates until he settled into a teaching job he had accepted there. The different birth dates on his Social Security card and immigration application were explained by his attorney. In his native Somalia, Kariye had lied about his birth date to avoid conscription by the communist government. He was working on behalf of Islamic Resistance—the guys the United States backed at the time. He made the mistake of stating his correct birthday on his Social Security card application.

Kariye's mosque had been infiltrated by an undercover FBI asset. His sermons and private conversations had been taped. A surveillance plane had flown over his mosque. His associates had been tailed and questioned. Yet the government couldn't make a case against him. "At that point, the government should have said, 'We're sorry. You can go,' " said his lawyer Stanley Cohen. "But U.S. attorneys don't think like that." They prosecuted Kariye for lying about his date of birth on his Social Security application. And for understating his income so his children could qualify for the Oregon Health Plan. He spent five weeks in jail.

After sinking a quarter of a million dollars in an investigation and prosecution that netted $5,109 in restitution, a $1,000 fine, and a five-year probated sentence, a federal prosecutor said with a straight face: "At least we established that one of the state's most prominent religious leaders had lied about his income." He forgot to mention conflicting birth dates on two federal forms.

Steve Wax didn't want the U.S. attorneys to begin a prosecution they couldn't walk away from. Nor did he want his client to testify before a grand jury. At least not until he knew what the government had against Mayfield. That was another problem. Courts are level playing fields because each side has access to the evidence the other side does. Those of us who couldn't get into law school learned that from watching *My Cousin Vinny*, in which the hapless defense attorney Vinny Gambini is stunned when a prosecutor hands over the case file of Gambini's murder defendant. "It's called disclosure, you dickhead. He has to give it to you," says his girlfriend, Mona Lisa Vito.

After 9/11, the playing field is no longer level. Steve Wax

didn't have the discovery process Vinny Gambini did. Some of the government's evidence against Brandon Mayfield was gathered by a secret FISA warrant. Some of what the government had was obscured in the redacted sections of the Werder affidavit. And additional secret information was in the U.S. attorneys' files. Because Mayfield was a material witness and not a defendant, the rules of discovery didn't apply.

To complicate matters, another expert witness in San Francisco had agreed with the FBI on Latent Fingerprint 17. Wax had paid the expert witness with public defender's funding, so the defense would "own" his report. But the finding made it more difficult for Judge Jones to release Mayfield, who asked to be allowed to go home and work while wearing an electronic ankle bracelet.

Nothing was working for Mayfield. The proceedings in the courtroom and everything about them were supposed to be secret. But somehow Mayfield's arrest as a material witness, his identity, and the terrorist crime his government was trying to hang on him were big news. The day before he was arrested in Oregon, the Department of Justice decided to leak his story back in Washington. The Justice Department had turned Mayfield's arrest into a public relations victory. Reporters in Washington were all over the secret proceedings. Tom Nelson's office took a call from *Newsweek*'s Michael Isikoff while Mayfield was making his first appearance before the judge. As did Judge Jones. On the night of the arrest, Isikoff told the story on *Nightline*. As the world's attention turned toward Portland, Mona Mayfield and her three children were trapped in their house, where TV stations set up satellite trucks on the street and reporters stormed the house any time she stepped in front of a door or window.

"Some time ago, some weeks ago, Spanish authorities presented the FBI with some evidence showing that the fingerprints found on a bag containing bomb material connected with the Spanish bombing was, in fact, from a Portland, Oregon, lawyer, a man by the name of Brandon Mayfield. He's an American convert to Islam," Isikoff said.

"He had popped up in connection [with] the Portland Seven case. That is the case of the seven individuals charged with plotting to go to Afghanistan after September 11 to fight for the Taliban against U.S. soldiers. Mr. Mayfield had represented the interests of one of the main defendants in that case. . . .

"But this was taken extremely seriously by the FBI. He's been on around the clock surveillance. . . . We learned about it from law enforcement sources."

Agence France-Presse had the story, from an official and anonymous source in Washington. *The Oregonian* had the story, attributed to a law enforcement official. Mayfield's hometown paper in Wichita, Kansas, had the story the day after his arrest, attributing their report to two senior law enforcement officials.

Justice Department sources weren't just leaking. They were running a media campaign that put Mayfield at risk when he was moved out of solitary confinement and into the general jailhouse population, where his fellow inmates recognized the "terrorist" from the TV news reports they watched in jail.

"How dare they?" asked Wax, the only time the cautious lawyer became animated during an interview. "How could they do this in a secret proceeding with a man who had not been charged?"

Courtroom TV dramas—from *Perry Mason* to *Boston Legal*—are built around the premise that there is drama in the courtroom. Dramatic moments in court are, in fact, rare. In Brandon Mayfield's secret detention, the dramatic moment was stunning. On the afternoon of May 20, 2004, two weeks after Mayfield first appeared in court, U.S. attorney Charles Gorder called to request a meeting with the judge and Mayfield's attorneys. Gorder told the judge the Spanish National Police had arrested an Algerian whose fingerprint matched Latent Print 17. Steve Wax didn't recall the judge barking out any order. "He almost said it with his eyes," Wax said. All parties were in court for Mayfield's release the following day.

"Basically," Gorder said at the May 20 hearing, "the Spanish government has informed us they have identified print No. 17, which the FBI lab and the Court expert had matched to Mr. Mayfield's prints, as belonging to another individual in Spain. . . . In light of this information, it is our request that Mr. Mayfield be released pending further proceedings in this material witness proceeding." It turned out that the print was not even an index finger, though the FBI match described it as a 100 percent match of Mayfield's right index.

Steve Wax said that the system worked. And that Judge Jones had moved with "lightning speed," considering that federal prosecutors had hard forensic evidence they were using to convince the court that they had an international terrorist in custody. But Mayfield's house had been searched in what seemed like a clear violation of the Fourth Amendment. He had been detained without just cause. Private case files of his clients—many of them Muslims with an understandable fear of their government—had been reviewed by the government and were photocopied and retained by the FBI. Mayfield had only spent two weeks in jail, but during that two weeks his law practice began to unravel.

Even the Mayfield kids had been involved. "Spanish documents" the agents had used to link Mayfield to Spain were his son's Spanish homework. The Internet links to Spanish websites were also Spanish assignments and Mona Mayfield's search for a program where her kids might study abroad. What the FBI described as Mayfield's radical quote supporting the Taliban was two sentences from his ten-year-old daughter Sharia's journal. Even if Mayfield had shouted it out in Portland's Pioneer Courthouse Square, it hardly seems like probable cause. Sharia had written, "Who is America to bomb the Taliban because they don't like

Afghanistan's law? All I say is that Americans should think twice about the example you are setting for the rest of the countries."

What would have been an insult to Mayfield, had it not provided him complete vindication, was the FBI's admission that their copy of the fingerprint from Madrid was in fact "of no value for identification purposes."

Mayfield continues his daily prayers at the Bilal Mosque, also known as the Intel Mosque. Many of the men who worship there are Intel engineers from Pakistan, India, and Southeast Asia. You know, the guys who are making technological progress happen in this country.

"Brandon Mayfield was fortunate," his friend Tom Nelson said. "His detention was based on one piece of hard evidence, which his attorneys could challenge. It's much harder for people detained as material witnesses on circumstantial evidence, which is harder to disprove."

"Our government took a dump on the Bill of Rights," Brandon Mayfield told a reporter after he was released. The comment embarrassed his daughter, Sharia.

POSTSCRIPT

Released from jail, with his law practice damaged and his family traumatized, Brandon Mayfield decided to pursue a day in court on terms he would better understand. He retained Gerry Spence, a legendary Wyoming trial lawyer, and filed a joint and several liability suit against the agents of government who had targeted him. Named as defendants were Agent Richard Werder and the latent print examiners Terry Green, John T. Massey, and Michael T. Wieners, who together make a compelling argument for outsourcing all FBI forensics to Spain. Also named were John Does I through X, in case any other responsible parties were turned up in discovery. Mayfield's first break came when the case was moved from federal court in Portland to Eugene, because the judge to whom it was assigned in Portland had once disparaged Gerry Spence before a group of lawyers attending a continuing legal education session. The case was reassigned to Ann Aiken, a thoughtful, evenhanded judge appointed to the federal bench by Bill Clinton.

Spence set out to look at the FBI's fingerprint analysis and the honesty of the agents involved in the case. "From the newspaper, it was clear to us that somebody was lying because the FBI had told the federal judge here in Portland in a sworn affidavit that the Spanish police agreed with the fingerprint match, yet [the Spanish police] were being quoted in *The New York Times* that they never said that," said Elden Rosenthal, an Oregon lawyer working with Spence. Mayfield's attorneys also set out to prove that the government had leaked information to the press and abused the Privacy Act. And they began building a challenge to some of the provisions of the Patriot Act.

Mayfield never made it to court.

When the judge overruled the government's motion for summary dismissal, the FBI folded. The government agreed to a $2 million settlement and an apology, though denying that Mayfield was targeted because he was a Muslim. In settling the case, government lawyers admitted that what had happened to Mayfield was "deeply unsettling." Anyone looking at the general contours of the case could understand why the agency couldn't open its files to lawyers.

"I think they settled the case because we were about to take in-depth discovery about what they do and how they do it and who may have violated Privacy Act provisions, which carry severe penalties," said Rosenthal.

The FBI always claims it has never misidentified a fingerprint, and prints are often the unassailable bedrock evidence upon which government lawyers prove out their cases. Exposing that process to the harsh light of a federal courtroom would have provided defense lawyers with grounds for challenging one of the agency's most basic tools. So the government settled.

Remarkably, Mayfield and his attorneys preserved their right to challenge the Patriot Act provision that opened the doors of his house to secret search by the FBI. The Patriot Act had so lowered the standard required to secretly enter an individual's home that agents could wink and nod and a judge would issue a warrant. Under FISA, the Foreign Intelligence Surveillance Act, federal agents could secretly wiretap someone's home only after convincing a FISA court judge that the target is an agent of a foreign power and the primary purpose of the wiretap is to gather intelligence. Under the Patriot Act, gathering intelligence only has to be a "significant purpose." Before they finished their business, the agency had taken three hundred photos, DNA samples, hair samples, and cigarette butts and kept the family—perhaps in their most intimate moments—under electronic surveillance. Mayfield is going back to court to argue that if the FBI is going to use the Patriot Act to conduct domestic criminal investigations, the bureau must comply with the search and seizure provisions of the Fourth Amendment.

Even before the suit was settled, the FBI was forced to admit that in its investigation of Mayfield it had for the first time used FISA and the sneak-and-peek provision of the Patriot Act to spy on an American citizen in his home.

Gerry Spence wants that provision declared unconstitutional. He wants the government to go to court and make its case before a judge if it plans to plant bugs in a citizen's home or office. He wants former AG John Ashcroft to pay damages for his policies. Speaking to reporters on the day of the settlement, Spence suggested why Americans should be concerned with the Patriot Act: "We have some secret agents who file secret papers that we can never see. And they're filed in a secret proceeding, and no right is given to the citizens. And out of those secret papers comes a secret order. And then people come secretly to your house, and they secretly break into your house. And they secretly put in listening devices. So that secretly the entire lives of these people become the property—not of us, not of the parties, not of the citizens—but our private lives become the property of the United States government."

It reads like a passage right out of Kafka.

SIX

Roe v. Doe

Democracy abhors undue secrecy, in recognition that public knowledge secures freedom.

—Judge Victor Marrero, October 2004

Had I been allowed to talk to the Senate or House while they were renewing the Patriot Act, I wanted them to explain to me how they perceived the distinction between a police force authorized to operate in secret and a secret police. Because I didn't see the distinction myself.

—John Doe, April 2007

One of the commonplace perversities of totalitarian societies is the manufacturing of official truth—an endeavor that requires persistent attention to detail. In Milan Kundera's *The Unbearable Lightness of Being*, fictitious Czechoslovak apparatchiks bungle their attempt to turn a small-town mayor into a "nonperson" when they inadvertently leave his black bowler hat in place after airbrushing him out of a photograph. The bowler floating above a gap in a line of sober dignitaries is a permanent reminder of the mendacity by which the government survives.

In January 2006 *New York Times* reporter Alison Leigh Cowan filed a story from a San Antonio hotel ballroom, where one citizen's absence was as absurd as the man missing beneath the floating bowler in Kundera's novel.

Cowan wasn't writing fiction.

Her story on the American Library Association's winter meeting was as nuanced as anything you could have read in the Czechoslovak press after the Soviet Army smothered the democratic promise of Prague Spring in 1968.

Cowan was covering a banquet where the recipient of the annual intellectual freedom award was "John Doe." His identity, if revealed, could result in his immediate imprisonment. Or the imprisonment of anyone who revealed it. Yet everyone in the room knew who John Doe was, even if they didn't know the identity of the FBI agent described in one court document as "John Roe," who had handed John Doe a national security letter that included a perpetual gag order.

John Doe had gone to court to fight the demands and gag order conveyed in the letter. In court filings responding to that request, the government failed to redact the name of the organization for which John Doe worked: the Library Connection of Windsor, Connecticut. Once the government's sloppy redaction revealed that name, which the government insisted was a national security secret, Cowan tracked down its director and executive board members. One or all of them had to be John Doe. But by identifying John Doe, Cowan herself might have been subject to arrest. So she wrote around the story, arriving at a circumspect conclusion:

> Alice S. Knapp, a Stamford librarian who is this year's president of the Connecticut Library Association, said she was there

> "taking pictures left and right." But the Library Connection's executive director, George Christian, and the vice president of its board, Peter Chase, did not attend. Mr. Chase's absence was especially odd since he was to be the Connecticut Library Association's advocate on intellectual freedom this year.
>
> Without commenting on John Doe's likely identity, Ms. Knapp confirmed that she had assumed many of Mr. Chase's speaking duties this year. For moral support, she has been nominating John Doe for other awards.

Wink wink.

Nod nod.

George Christian and Peter Chase were John Doe 1 and John Doe 2. Christian, in fact, was the recipient of the intellectual freedom award being handed out in San Antonio that night. On the advice of his attorney, he stayed at home in Hartford, aware that he could be arrested for walking onto the stage to pick up his five-hundred-dollar check and plaque.

The Roe v. Doe story began on July 8, 2005, when Christian got a call from an employee he supervised. An FBI agent had called to ask who could receive service of a national security letter addressed to the Library Connection, which provides computer services for twenty-six Connecticut libraries. As executive director, Christian was responsible for the organization's legal affairs. The letter should be directed to him.

The following week, two FBI officers showed up in Christian's office. He was handed a letter demanding electronic records that would determine who had used a library computer between 4:00 and 4:45 P.M. on a specific day six months earlier. Christian's background is in corporate IT. He was hired to design and run the systems that provide computer services and electronic data preservation to the libraries that fund the consortium. He understood what the agents wanted and knew why he couldn't provide it.

"I told the agent he was out of luck," Christian said. "When a computer is turned on, a router assigns it to an IP address, and the routers use address translation to hide the computers behind them—if only to make hacking more difficult." The specific information wasn't available unless all the information on every library patron was turned over to the FBI. The agents were looking for an electronic needle in a haystack.

"Don't worry, we've got ways," Agent Aram Crandall replied. He told Christian to pull the information together and comply with the demand stated in the letter.

While two FBI agents waited in Christian's office, he read the third paragraph of his national security letter, which cited a statute and certified that the information the agent had requested was "relevant to an authorized investigation against international terrorism or clandestine intelligence activities, and that such an investigation of a United States person is not conducted solely on the basis of activities protected by the first amendment to the Constitution of the United States."

Christian had never heard of a national security letter. He says he would have cooperated if he believed there was a genuine and immediate terrorist threat. It was July 8. The letter was dated May 19. Almost a week had passed since the FBI had called his office. The letter was not even addressed to him but to the Library Connection employee FBI agents had initially contacted.

"This didn't look like the FBI was in hot pursuit of anyone," Christian said.

The third paragraph of the letter prohibited the recipient from "disclosing to any person that the FBI has sought or obtained access or information to [*sic*] records under these provisions."

Christian took a risk.

"I told the agent I didn't think the statute was constitutional," he said. "And that I was going to discuss it with my attorney." The agent wrote a private phone number on the back of his card and told Christian to have the attorney call him.

Christian made up his mind that he wasn't going to comply before the agents walked out of his office. He called the Library Connection's attorney, whose work is focused on keeping non-profits in compliance with federal and state law. "She had never heard of a national security letter," Christian said. "She had never seen those three words used together like that." The lawyer assigned several law students the task of researching national security letters. When they completed their research, she told Christian he was in a real bind. Denying the FBI's demands would entail taking on the "attorney general of the United States." Christian called the consortium's vice president, Peter Chase, and requested an emergency meeting of the executive board.

Peter Chase is the librarian from central casting. Soft-spoken, dignified, and earnest, he is the director of the town library of Plainville, Connecticut (pop. 17,000, 90,000 volumes). He is also a ferocious defender of the privacy, and what he describes as the "intellectual rights," of his patrons. Chase never had any doubt that the Library Connection would refuse to comply with the FBI's request for records. What his lawyer told him strengthened his resolve.

"They were going after our patrons with a national security letter?" Chase said. "Our lawyer told us the targets of national security letters don't even have to be suspected of any criminal activity themselves. And the FBI doesn't have to show anyone that this investigation has anything to do with national security.

"There is no oversight. When we heard that, we said no, no, no! We're not going to do this."

Their attorney put them in touch with the American Civil Liberties Union, whose attorneys Ann Beeson and Jameel Jaffer drove up to Connecticut from New York to meet the librarians. Beeson said she didn't feel secure discussing the case over the phone. The lawyers told no one in their office where they were going, fearing an inadvertent leak might result in charges filed against them and their prospective clients. It was not clear that a recipient of a national security letter could speak to a lawyer without breaking the law. "There was a real risk," Beeson said. "We had seen the FBI play hardball with our other [national security letter] client. We would like to think they wouldn't act that way with these folks. But you never know."

Beeson's other national security letter client, a John Doe plaintiff, is the owner of a small Internet access and consulting business in New York. He had won a lower court ruling nine months earlier, when a federal judge ruled that the national security letter that John Doe had received violated his First Amendment and Fourth Amendment protections.

To say John Doe won is an understatement. Federal district judge Victor Marrero wrote a 120-word opinion that declared national security letters violations of Fourth Amendment protections against search and seizure and the First Amendment guarantee of free speech. Under the law governing the use of national security letters, as modified by the Patriot Act in 2001, the FBI could compel a recipient to produce documents or electronic files with no opportunity to challenge the demand in court. Searches and seizures, the judge wrote, "must be performed pursuant to a valid warrant based upon probable cause," which requires approval by a judge. Yet NSLs were being issued by any one of fifty-six supervisors in regional FBI offices. And there was nothing in the letters that even implied that a recipient could challenge an NSL in court.

"The literal terms of the non-disclosure order," the judge wrote, "would bar the recipient from even consulting with an attorney to file such a challenge." To go to court is to break the law. "Even if he were to challenge the NSL on his own, the recipient would necessarily have to disclose the fact of the NSL's issuance to the clerk of the court and to the presiding judge, again, in violation of the literal terms of the non-disclosure provision," wrote Judge Marrero in a blistering, indignant opinion.

The government had argued that the nondisclosure provision didn't stop John Doe from hiring a lawyer. But Judge Marrero observed that thousands of NSLs had been issued since they were authorized in 1986 and not one recipient had ever challenged a letter until John Doe showed up in court. The judge also had a problem with a perpetual gag order that "presupposes a class of speech, that, for reasons not satisfactorily explained, must forever be kept from public view, cloaked by an official order that will always overshadow the public's right to know."

"Democracy," Judge Marrero wrote, "abhors undue secrecy, in recognition that public knowledge secures freedom."

The ACLU attorneys representing their invisible client had hit the ball out of the park. Or out of the federal courtroom in Manhattan. The judge stayed his decision for ninety days, to allow the government time to submit motions to protect sensitive information that might be compromised by his orders. And he observed that some possible legislative fixes were moving through Congress. But he ruled that an FBI agent walking into someone's office with a letter that demanded private information, gagged the recipient *forever*, denied access to an attorney, and provided no recourse to a judge was flatly unconstitutional. Which in another time would have seemed like an exercise in judicial moderation.

The government appealed, and while the case was on appeal, the ACLU attorneys in New York got the call from Connecticut.

To the ACLU the Library Connection case was timely. While Beeson and Jaffer sat down to listen with the librarians in Connecticut, Congress was debating and revising the Patriot Act. John Doe New York was gagged and in the middle of an appeal, unable to testify before Congress or even speak to a member of Congress about his experience. Attorney General Alberto Gonzales was reassuring the public that the Patriot Act was not being used to go after libraries. United States attorneys across the nation were out selling the repackaged Patriot Act before any forum that would listen. And four librarians from Connecticut, whose experience with the law contradicted most of what most of its proponents were describing, were forbidden to tell their story, even to their elected representatives in Washington.

The librarians signed a retainer agreement with the ACLU attorneys, and the ACLU signed on to the case as both counsel and co-plaintiffs. They filed suit in federal court, making the same Fourth, Fifth, and First Amendment arguments they had made on behalf of John Doe New York. Their most urgent request was an immediate preliminary injunction that would allow their clients to speak about their experience with a national security letter.

The assistant U.S. attorney defending the government went, to use a lay term, ballistic. To disclose that the Library Connection had received a national security letter would jeopardize national security, argued Lisa Perkins. The subject who had used library computers would be tipped off. Terrorists working in American libraries would be made aware that the FBI was looking over their shoulders and adapt their tactics to avoid surveillance. An instrument Congress had authorized to fight terrorism would be undermined.

The case was tried under the highest national security standards, with every document filed under seal and scrutinized by U.S. attorneys, who would redact much of the information before turning it over to the court, where it would become part of the public record. The librarians would remain gagged for the duration of their trial, prohibited from telling family members and employees that they had received an NSL. There were also two Jane Does, Barbara Bailey and Janet Nocek, also Library Connection board members. The two women were less prominent, Bailey said, because the media quickly figured out the identities of

George Christian and Peter Chase. She said it was very difficult, however, to conceal her situation from her husband. Absent their spouses, who could not be told of the lawsuit, the librarians watched their district court hearing, which took place in a federal courtroom in Bridgeport, from a secure room in the federal courthouse in Hartford on closed-circuit TV, unable to communicate with the judge or their attorneys.

Even the evidence used against them was top secret. The FBI's demand for their library records was based on a classified file that could not be made public without putting national security at risk. The librarians, their lawyers, and the judge would have to trust that the threat to national security was serious enough to warrant gagging the librarians *for the rest of their lives.*

Something in that argument didn't pass Judge Janet C. Hall's smell test. A Bill Clinton appointee, she'd gone from law school to an international law firm, worked as a trial attorney and special U.S. attorney at the Department of Justice, then become a partner at a Connecticut office of a large firm. She quickly came up with a Solomonic solution regarding the classified evidence. She had her own high-level security clearance, obtained before she was appointed to the federal bench. She announced that she would read the classified file in her chamber.

She was not impressed with what she read.

"Judge Hall wrote a give-me-a-break opinion," said Beeson.

The judge found nothing in the classified files or the arguments of the government's attorneys that justified suspending the librarians' First Amendment rights. She seemed offended that the FBI would make such a demand. She stopped short of ordering the librarians to catch the next Acela to Washington and tell their story to the Congress. But she was clearly disturbed by the agency's contempt for the First Amendment.

She also rather discreetly called the FBI agents and the former attorney general, well, liars. Ashcroft, in the instance cited by the judge, had engaged not in genteel dissembling but in outright lying complemented with a crude insult. The ban on the librarians' speech was "particularly noteworthy," Judge Hall wrote, because Patriot Act proponents had reassured the public—and librarians in particular—that the act was being narrowly applied. The judge quoted a speech Attorney General John Ashcroft had made in Memphis in 2003, when he ridiculed librarians, "accusing those who fear executive abuse of increased access to library records under the PATRIOT Act of 'hysteria' and stating that 'the Department of Justice has neither the staffing, the time nor the inclination to monitor the reading habits of Americans.' "

(Judge Hall didn't fully capture the flavor of Ashcroft's speech, in which he seemed to be channeling the late and rhetorically overblown Spiro Agnew: "The charges of the hysterics are revealed for what they are, castles in the air built on misrepresentation, supported by unfounded fear, held aloft by hysteria. . . . The fact is, with just 11,000 FBI agents and over a billion visitors to America's libraries each year, the Department of Justice has neither the staffing, the time nor the inclination to monitor the reading habits of Americans. No offense to the American Library Association, but we just don't care.")

The Patriot Act was up for renewal, Judge Hall wrote, and "the very people who might have information regarding investigative abuses and overreaching are preemptively prevented from sharing that information with the legislators who empower the executive branch with the tools used to investigate matters of national security."

If George Christian had been George Tenet, he might have called Judge Hall's opinion "a slam dunk."

The government appealed and got an automatic stay on the decision, and the four librarians from Hartford found themselves stuck in a through-the-looking-glass judicial process.

They had already shredded, hidden, or destroyed any paperwork, correspondence, or electronic files related to their national security letter. They had to hide their role in the lawsuit from their spouses, children, family members, and friends; should anyone learn about the national security letter and even inadvertently leak the information, he would be subject to prosecution and prison. "It was the last thing you would want to expose your loved one to," said an earnest Peter Chase, left to describe a government document as if it were the AIDS virus.

Several days before Judge Hall handed down her decision, Alison Leigh Cowan, the enterprising *New York Times* reporter who had pored over the court records, called Chase at home. She began her phone interview with an innocuous question about his work as chair of the Connecticut Library Association. When Cowan asked Chase if he had seen the trial in Hartford, he panicked. A cannot-tell-a-lie kind of guy, Chase knew the reporter had been in the courtroom and was aware the plaintiffs weren't there. If he answered yes, he would by default admit that he was one of the plaintiffs who'd watched from a remote site. He hung up, confirming her suspicion. The Library Connection plaintiffs were required to report any contact with the media, so Chase called his attorneys in New York. They told him he had to leave town. If the *Times* identified him in a story, he would be besieged by reporters. And perhaps by the FBI, who would be able to obtain his phone records and verify that he'd had an extended conversation with a *New York Times* reporter. Chase's attorneys in New York retained a criminal defense lawyer to represent him, and Chase told his wife they were leaving earlier than planned for their Labor Day vacation.

He didn't tell her why.

By November, Cowan reported that the Library Connection was the recipient of the NSL. "As government secrets go, this one did not take long to unravel," she wrote. Though the government was engaged in what might described as *redactio ad absurdum*, it had failed to redact its own court filing. Cowan's account of the sloppy handling of what the FBI considered national security secrets made the government legal team look like Keystone counsel:

> It was right there, in bold type, on Page 7 of an Aug. 16 memorandum of law, in between black splotches applied by government censors to wipe out hints of the organization's identity.
>
> It was also on Page 18 of the memo, and it was visible in the header line on a court Web site to anyone who looked up the case using the file number.
>
> The name of the organization was so evident, both through telltale clues and explicit references, that *The New York Times* published it six times in news reports on the continuing court case, and it was named in other publications as well. Yet the federal government continues to argue in federal courts in Bridgeport, Manhattan and Washington that the identity of Library Connection, a consortium of libraries, must be kept secret, in the interest of rooting out potential terrorists. A decision from the United States Court of Appeals for the Second Circuit, in New York, could come soon.

(You can almost hear *The Daily Show*'s Jon Stewart screaming, "Look, look, it was everywhere!")

The government's redactors had bungled the most basic tasks of redaction, inadvertently revealing the name of the secret recipient of the NSL. And Ann Beeson believed that the elaborate ruse had run its course and the librarians would easily prevail in the Second Court of Appeals in New York. "I thought it would be a no-brainer," she said. "We thought we wouldn't even have to file papers. We thought we'd call the judge on the Second Circuit and say, 'I guess you read the paper today, and don't you want to talk?' And instead they forced us to brief the whole thing."

Black Panther Bobby Seale had been bound and gagged in the courtroom when Judge Julius Hoffman tried the Chicago Eight (which became the Chicago Seven when Hoffman sent Seale to prison for contempt of court) in 1969. The Hartford Four were gagged and invisible—even if anyone paying attention to the *Times* and half a dozen other media outlets knew Christian and Chase by name, though the *Times* couldn't report that they were John Does without itself breaking the law.

Although their organization's name had been revealed, Christian and Chase (and executive board members Barbara Bailey and Janet Nocek) were forced to continue the invisible-plaintiff charade throughout the appeals process, under threat of prosecution should they reveal that the Library Connection had received an NSL, which, of course, had already been revealed by the *Times*. When the ACLU attorneys attached a copy of *The New York Times* to a motion they filed, the government, in a hearing closed to the public, insisted that the *Times* article had to be redacted. And although the cat was out of the bag, Department of Justice attorneys insisted on redacting the phrase "the cat is out of the bag" from pleadings filed by the ACLU attorneys.

"It was an oral argument in a closed courtroom," Beeson said. "The level of secrecy was absurd. The *Times* articles were completely redacted. You couldn't even see '*New York Times*.' "

When a hearing was finally scheduled in open court in New York in November 2005, the Connecticut librarians were allowed to attend only if they agreed to strict conditions that would preserve their anonymity. Oral arguments on their appeal would be held in a large federal courthouse with several courtrooms, so they could sit in the courtroom rather than a remote location, although they could not enter the courtroom together, sit together, speak or make eye contact with each other or their attorneys while in the courtroom. And they had to leave separately.

The case was argued with most of its content elided, which

must have bewildered two dozen judges from Peru, outfitted with headsets that allowed them to listen to simultaneous translation as they observed how jurisprudence is done in the big leagues. Something was lost in translation.

"Revealing our identities was a national security threat?" said Peter Chase. "There were librarians from Connecticut all over the courtroom, and every one of them knew I was John Doe."

The Connecticut case had been consolidated with John Doe New York's case. But one difference remained between the two. Everyone except the Peruvian judges knew that the Library Connection had received an NSL and that George Christian and Peter Chase were almost certainly John Does 1 and 2 from Connecticut. The hearing became a courtroom version of Where's Waldo? as the Connecticut John and Jane Does looked around the room trying to guess who was the New York John Doe while the New York John Doe looked around the courtroom trying to guess who the Connecticut John and Jane Does were.

Despite the manifest absurdity of national security secrets that could be found in *The New York Times* and anonymous plaintiffs whose identities were widely known, the appellate court judges refused to lift the gag on the librarians. "That's why we took the radical, or somewhat radical, action of going to the Supreme Court with an emergency motion," Beeson said.

Supreme Court justice Ruth Bader Ginsburg's opinion, some of which was redacted and classified, was sympathetic with the "anomaly" the librarians confronted: "Doe—the only entity in a position to impart a first-hand account of his experience—remains barred from revealing its identity, while others who obtained knowledge of Doe's identity—when the cat was inadvertently let out of the bag—may speak freely on the subject."

Although Justice Ginsburg used the previously redacted phrase "cat . . . let out of the bag," she refused to lift the gag order on the librarians.

Beeson was stunned. "I'm not even sure when the last time—I mean the fact that the Supreme Court issued a decision that was classified—there was any example of this. Or if there was any other example. Other judges in cases regarding secrecy assumed that they would have to do everything in their power to avoid issuing any part of a decision that was not available to the public."

The highest court in the country had ruled that the librarians would not be able to relate their experience to members of Congress who were considering renewing the very provision that had the librarians gagged.

On one occasion, Peter Chase had to decline an invitation from the League of Women Voters to debate U.S. attorney Kevin O'Connor on the merits of the Patriot Act—because he had been gagged by U.S. attorney Kevin O'Connor. (O'Connor went ahead with his half of the debate.)

Then the FBI folded. After nine months of hardball litigation, the government lifted the gag order and dropped the demand for computer records. "Their timing was sinister," said Chase. A far better choice of word than "cynical." Approximately two weeks after President Bush signed the renewed Patriot Act, the John Does of Connecticut were free to call their senators and representatives. "After the revised Patriot Act was signed into law," Chase said, "the government suddenly decided that our identity was not really a security threat after all and that our gag should be lifted. Nothing had changed in the case, so what happened to the threat to national security?"

"They also took away our standing," Chase said. There was no reason to go to court to fight when there was nothing to contest. Ann Beeson said that's correct in a purely technical sense. They could have continued the fight. But John Doe New York, who remained gagged, provided a better vehicle to advance the claim that the government's use of national security letters is a violation of the Bill of Rights.

To the government, the librarians were now irrelevant. They had been gagged long enough to keep them out of the public debate of the law that kept them gagged. John Doe New York's case was remanded back to Judge Marrero's courtroom to be retried, taking into consideration the changes Congress had made in the Patriot Act.

Congress had made some improvements in the act. Recipients of national security letters would be allowed to consult an attorney. There was now a process by which NSL recipients could go to court to challenge the FBI. And the penalty for violating the terms of an NSL—five years in federal prison—was spelled out so that anyone who might violate the law wouldn't be left in the dark.

The most cynical, or perhaps "sinister," reform eliminated the perpetual gag order while at the same time keeping it in place. Recipients of NSLs can now go to court to challenge their gag orders at one-year intervals after the first-year anniversary of the letter. But there's a catch. Judges are required to accept as conclusive the FBI argument that a specific gag remains essential to national security. Call it the Judge Hall amendment. No judge can lift a gag unless the FBI agrees it can be lifted.

Six months after the Second Court of Appeals sent John Doe New York back to Judge Marrero's court for a new trial, the inspector general of the Department of Justice released a report that documented the volume of NSLs the FBI had issued between 2003 and 2005: 44,000 NSLs containing 142,074 requests, in one investigation demanding information relating to 11,000 telephone numbers. The report excoriated the FBI for its abuse of NSLs—and exigent letters intended to be used in the most dire circumstances, such as a kidnapping or an imminent threat. Many of the letters had been issued in violation of the agency's own guidelines.

At about the same time, Connecticut's U.S. attorney, Kevin

O'Connor, got a promotion. He was called to Washington to replace Kyle Sampson, the young deputy to Attorney General Alberto Gonzales who resigned because of his role in the partisan firing of U.S. attorneys who weren't considered "loyal Bushies." Telegenic and aggressive, with degrees from Notre Dame and the University of Connecticut law school, O'Connor is expected to return to Connecticut to run for elected office.

SEVEN

Our Time in the Shadows

Excessive bail shall not be required, nor excessive fines imposed, nor cruel and unusual punishments inflicted.

—Eighth Amendment to the United States Constitution

In all criminal prosecutions, the accused shall enjoy the right to a speedy and public trial, by an impartial jury of the State and district wherein the crime shall have been committed, which district shall have been previously ascertained by law, and to be informed of the nature and cause of the accusation; to be confronted with the witnesses against him; to have compulsory process for obtaining witnesses in his favor, and to have the Assistance of Counsel for his defence.

—Sixth Amendment to the United States Constitution

We also have to work, though, sort of the dark side, if you will. We've got to spend time in the shadows in the intelligence world. . . . That's the world these folks operate in, and so it's going to be vital for us to use any means at our disposal, basically, to achieve our objective.

—Vice President Dick Cheney, September 16, 2001

In Kandahar, they hanged me by my hands. For hours, sometimes for days.

—Murat Kurnaz, June 21, 2007

Fifteen American soldiers watched over one man shackled to a seat in the cargo bay of a C-17 Globemaster—the Air Force workhorse that transports Abrams tanks, Chinook helicopters, and infantry vehicles. Wearing goggles that shut out all light, a soundproof headset, and a mask that covered his mouth so he could not speak, spit, or bite, the prisoner arrived at Ramstein Air Base in Kaiserslautern, Germany, under the tightest security. The plane had burned through 36,000 gallons of jet fuel and refueled in flight. During the seventeen-hour, bone-chilling ride in the yawning cargo bay, the prisoner was provided neither food nor water. Nor was he allowed to stretch his legs or relieve himself.

This was how what had been the world's greatest democracy when George Bush took the presidential oath in 2001 repatriated an innocent man who never represented a security threat to the United States. Murat Kurnaz was nineteen when he was taken off a bus in Peshawar, Pakistan. He was twenty-four and the last European held at the American prison camp in Cuba when he was flown to Kaiserslautern in August 2006. He didn't know he had been returned home to Germany until an American enlisted man removed the goggles and Kurnaz saw three German policemen standing outside the airplane.

"He was dumped on German soil like some sort of alien," said Bernhard Docke, Kurnaz's attorney from the northern German city of Bremen.

Murat Kurnaz, German born of Turkish parents, could be an expert witness and fact witness for any legislative or judicial procedure that would cast a cold eye on the transgressions of law, the Constitution, and the fundamental precepts of human rights perpetrated by George Bush's terror warriors. Pick your amendment. Fifth: not compelled to be a witness against yourself. Sixth: speedy and public trial and right to be confronted by witnesses.

Eighth: protection from cruel and unusual punishment. Fourteenth: the state cannot deprive someone of life, liberty, or property without due process of law. Constitutional right to habeas corpus? There might even be a First Amendment problem with locking a man up in an island prison and refusing to allow him to communicate with his family.

Kurnaz was Prisoner No. 53, the fifty-third detainee booked into Guantánamo. His four years and eight months in custody of the Central Intelligence Agency, the United States Army, Marine Corps, and Air Force, included an eclectic range of human rights abuses at the hands of his captors and torturers. Kurnaz could write a technical how-to-torture manual that would reassure Dick Cheney, David Addington, John Yoo, and federal judge Jay Bybee—the American public servants who made torture public policy—that their system works. How was this one man, pulled from a bus at a routine roadside stop near Peshawar, Pakistan, tortured by agents and soldiers whose salaries are paid by the United States Treasury?

Let us count the ways:

- routine physical beatings
- waterboarding (simulated drowning)
- sexual humiliation (fondled by and offered sex from female interrogators)
- electric shocks
- religious degradation by guards and interrogators who dragged or kicked the Qur'an across the floors of cells
- isolation in hot cells
- isolation in cold cells
- extended sleep deprivation followed by extended interrogation
- injection with drugs that cause drowsiness and disorientation
- suspension by his hands for days, while intermittently being interrogated.

Despite all this, Murat Kurnaz told his American torturers at Kandahar and Guantánamo nothing. Because he had nothing to tell them. His American captivity was the end result of a religious awakening common to first-generation Muslims in Germany, France, and the United Kingdom. Immigrant parents arrive in a country and assimilate, leaving their children with no cultural patrimony. And the children return to the kind of religious fundamentalism that San Antonio's Reverend John Hagee and Colorado Springs's Dr. James Dobson inspire in their disciples—the principal difference with Kurnaz being the text that informs the religious experience.

In Germany, the father had worked for thirty years at a Daimler plant in Bremen and drove a Mercedes. The son gave up his motorcycle, secular clothes, and jobs at a gym and a dance club and started spending time at an Arab mosque, where the lingua franca is the language of the Qur'an. Murat even persuaded his secular parents to connect him with family members in Turkey, who found him a traditional Muslim woman to marry.

The Abu Bakr mosque in Bremen was home to a small group of adherents of Jama'at al-Tablighi (the Party of Missionary Work), a worldwide Muslim revivalist group that insinuates itself into mosques. One of the followers of Jama'at al-Tablighi urged Kurnaz to go Pakistan, where he could study the Qur'an every day rather than one day a week. Selcuk Bilgin, another young Turk who found religion at Abu Bakr, decided to travel with him.

German bureaucratic efficiency started Kurnaz down the road alone to a chartered CIA aircraft ride from Kandahar to the American prison camp that Donald Rumsfeld set up ninety miles south of the reach of the American Constitution. Bilgin was detained at the airport in Frankfurt and never made the trip to Pakistan, because of an outstanding municipal fine he'd incurred by letting his dog run loose. So in October 2001, Murat Kurnaz was an itinerant fundamentalist Muslim whose traveling companion had been arrested in an airport. Both men lived in Bremen, an hour's drive from Hamburg, home to the al-Qaeda cell that plotted and carried out the 9/11 attack. And both had associated with Jama'at al-Tablighi. Those facts, and Dick Cheney's conviction that the Constitution is a document that can be selectively applied, got Murat Kurnaz almost five years of incarceration and torture at the hands of the American government.

The "privilege to a writ of habeas corpus" was a concession King John made when he signed the Magna Carta in 1215. The revolutionary concept that a prisoner can challenge his incarceration has since become part of the fabric of Anglo-American jurisprudence. Like free expression, it's a right that is required to secure all other rights. If a king or president—let's say Hugo Chávez or George Bush in the Americas, or Bashar al-Assad or Mahmoud Ahmadinejad in the Middle East—can have someone silenced or locked away with no legal route to freedom, other liberties guaranteed by a constitution don't mean much.

The "great writ" followed British subjects to thirteen American colonies, where it was sporadically observed. In Leonard W. Levy's *Origins of the Bill of Rights*, he describes a minor uprising in Ipswich, Massachusetts, in 1687, when a gang of unruly Ipswichers led by a preacher declared they would not pay new taxes imposed on them. Colonial governor Edmund Andros had the preacher and five of his followers thrown in prison. When they applied for a writ of habeas corpus, the judge denied it, telling them they must "not think the Laws of England follow them to the ends of the earth whither they went." A jury found the preacher and the Ipswich Five guilty, dismissing the argument that their imprisonment violated the Magna Carta. They got a stiff fine and no relief from the court.

This sort of high-handed behavior was on the minds of the framers of the Constitution when they met in 1787 in Philadelphia, where there was something of a habeas corpus feeding frenzy. South Carolina's Charles Pinckney proposed a near absolute right that the Congress could suspend only under the most "urgent and pressing occasion" and then only for a fixed time. Another South Carolinian, John Rutledge, argued that the right should never be suspended. James Wilson of Pennsylvania argued that suspension should never be necessary, and that any power to deny a writ of habeas corpus should rest with judges, who would decide on a case-by-case basis, not the Congress or the president ordering wholesale suspension.

Thomas Jefferson wrote home from his diplomatic posting in Paris, warning James Madison about insufficient attention to "the eternal unremitting force of the habeas corpus laws, and trials by jury." The right to habeas corpus was included in Article I of the Constitution, then reinforced in the Bill of Rights, by amendments that provide for a speedy public trial and prohibit excessive bail as well as cruel and unusual punishment.

The right was so powerfully reaffirmed by the Supreme Court in 1866 that the writ of habeas corpus seemed to become a writ writ in stone. The "fact situation" in the *Ex Parte Milligan* case wasn't complicated. What Abraham Lincoln described as "this mighty scourge of war" was grinding to its tragic conclusion when Lambden P. Milligan was caught in Indiana. He was plotting to seize a military garrison and arsenal, free the prisoners held there, and lead an insurrection. Milligan was tried and convicted by a military tribunal. The evidence suggests he was completely deserving of the hanging to which the military court sentenced him.

Lincoln could look out of the window of the White House and see General Robert E. Lee's plantation in Virginia at a moment when it was feared that Washington, D.C., would fall into the hands of the Confederacy. Yet the Supreme Court ruled that this civilian terrorist who never wore the uniform of the Union or the Confederacy had the right to habeas corpus and to be tried in a civilian court. All nine justices agreed. Domestic insurrection, a nation at war, a plan to violently assault a military compound. And Lambden P. Milligan had the constitutional right to a trial in a civilian court? It must have been a great country.

Writing for the majority of the Court, Justice David Davis looked back to the framers of our Constitution:

> Those great and good men foresaw that troublous times would arise, when rulers and people would become restive under restraint, and seek by sharp and decisive measures to accomplish ends deemed just and proper; and that the principles of constitutional liberty would be in peril, unless established by irrepealable law. The history of the world had taught them that what was done in the past might be attempted in the future. The Constitution of the United States is a law for rulers and people, equally in war and in peace, and covers with the shield of its protection all classes of men, at all times, and under all circumstances.

With the stroke of a pen, George W. Bush undid that high court decision and edited that magnificent paragraph.

A short, massive, muscular man with an unruly reddish beard splayed across his chest and hair pulled back in a ponytail, Murat Kurnaz speaks good, if basic, English. He says it improved in the years he spent at Kandahar and Guantánamo. He's a bit of a contradiction, a fundamentalist Muslim who drives a sports car and dresses like he selects his clothes from *GQ* ads. Kurnaz reluctantly agrees to interviews with reporters, though he earned a substantial amount of money for two exclusives with *Stern* magazine and a national television network soon after he returned to Germany from Guantánamo. He tends to end interviews abruptly with the same line: "I have to stop now."

In Pakistan, Kurnaz said he spent about two months traveling from city to city and mosque to mosque with a group of Jama'at al-Tablighi adherents. He was en route to catch a flight back to Germany when Pakistani police pulled him off a bus in December 2001. Initially the police told him he would be released to fly home. Then he was turned over to Americans.

In an interview in his lawyer's office in Bremen, and in follow-up telephone interviews, Kurnaz said that American interrogators initially asked him the whereabouts of Osama bin Laden. Again and again.

"Where is Osama?" he said. "Who is Osama?" "Do you know Osama?" "Are you a Taliban?" The questions were accompanied by beatings and electric shocks. The desperate line of questioning is understandable. Our country had just been devastated by terrorist attacks that were the result, in part, of intelligence failure. We had dispatched our intelligence agency and military to try to figure out what happened and what might be coming next, and Murat Kurnaz had ridden a bus into their path. For ten days, he was moved from place to place, shackled and with a sack over his head. Finally he was escorted onto an airplane. "Sit down, motherfucker" was the first thing he heard from the enlisted man who took charge of him.

He was flown to an American military base in Kandahar, where interrogations became more brutal and systematic. "I was hanged by my hands," he said. "Hanged for hours and sometimes days. Interrogators would come and then leave and come back." He said an American physician in camouflage would check his vital signs three times a day to determine if he could withstand more interrogation.

Kurnaz said he could hear a man on the other side of a partition and assumed he was being subjected to the same torture. On one occasion, Kurnaz saw him. "They were hanging me and pulled me up higher than the other times. I could see the man in the other room. He was hanging, too. Maybe they lifted him higher that time, too, I don't know. I had heard him moaning and breathing. This is the first time I saw him. He was dead. The color of his body was changed and I could see he was dead."

Kurnaz said that he was also subjected to waterboarding and electric shock. And that beatings were routine and constant. He suspects that much of the torture was a result of the failure of American soldiers and agents to capture any real terrorists in the initial sweeps. (He was told that the Pakistani police had sold him to the Americans for three thousand dollars.) "They didn't have any big fish. And they thought that by torture they could get one of us to say something. 'I know Osama' or something like that. Then they could say they had a big fish."

After two months in Kandahar, Kurnaz was shackled, hooded, and led to another plane. He said his captors told him they were taking him to the cave where Osama bin Laden was hiding, where he would be shot. The plane landed in Cuba.

At Guantánamo, a soldier who spoke German and would become a persistent tormentor said: "Do you know what the Germans did to the Jews? That's what we're going to do to you."

Kurnaz spent more than four years in Guantánamo, starting in Camp X-ray, the original temporary cages for inmates, and moving into permanent quarters after they were constructed. Much of his time was spent in isolation cells. In 2002, he said, he was moved into a completely closed, airless cell in Camp India, where he spent thirty-three consecutive days in what he describes as an oven.

After he was returned to Germany, Kurnaz wrote a book, with the assistance of German journalist and novelist Helmut Kuhn: *Fünf Jahre meines Lebens: Ein Bericht aus Guantanamo* (*Five Years of My Life: A Report from Guantánamo*). Others have been written, and more will follow. Genre torture narratives will become part of the legacy of the Bush-Cheney administration. It's not Solzhenitsyn. Told in terse, straightforward sentences and laced with mordant humor, *Five Years of My Life* makes compelling reading. It's being translated into English for an American release scheduled for 2008.

American movie rights have also been sold.

Asked about his religious practice, Kurnaz said he doesn't go to a mosque anymore. He won't say why. "I still pray," he said. "Not in a mosque."

Bernhard Docke is a tall, trim, elegant man who works at a small criminal defense law firm a few blocks from the train station in Bremen. In May 2002, Rabiya Kurnaz called him and asked for help. German law enforcement officials had shown up at her home in Bremen and told her they had good news and bad news regarding her oldest son, who had been missing for four months. The good news was that her son was alive. The bad news was that he was in American custody.

What followed was a four-year process to free Rabiya Kurnaz's son from what Docke refers to as a "tropical Bastille." (Bruce Fein, a constitutional lawyer who worked in the Reagan administration, uses this historical reference point in his bill of particulars supporting the impeachment of Vice President Dick Cheney. One impeachable offense Fein cites is Cheney's claim of "authority to detain American citizens as enemy combatants on the president's say-so alone, a frightening power indistinguishable from Louis XVI's execrated *lettres de cachet* that occasioned the storming of the Bastille.")

Docke described a desperate mother of a nineteen-year-old who had been told that there was no legal remedy for her son and that he might remain in prison indefinitely, or at least until the

American War on Terror was over. Rabiya Kurnaz had been to the American embassy to ask for help and was told to go to the German government. The Germans told her because she and her son were citizens of Turkey she should go to the Turkish embassy. At the Turkish embassy she was told her son's incarceration was an issue that would have to be addressed by the German and American governments.

"We were powerless," Docke said. He set out to establish that local law enforcement authorities had no record or criminal dossier that would link Kurnaz to any Islamist terrorist group that would justify his detention.

Docke paused.

"Nothing," he said. "Nothing justifies detention the way Murat was detained. And nothing justifies torture. You don't torture an innocent person. You don't even torture someone who is guilty."

Docke says the German government bears considerable responsibility for failing to act when the American government was torturing his client. "There are laws in Germany," he said. "The government is required by law to act when it is aware of torture."

Docke contacted the Center for Constitutional Rights, the New York public-interest law firm and advocacy group that coordinated litigation, recruited lawyers, and ultimately forced the United States Supreme Court to address the Guantánamo detentions. Before Murat Kurnaz was returned home to Germany, Docke would run up a twelve-hundred-hour tab, not including travel and expenses. Not all efforts were compensated, but he got financial support from the CCR, the American Civil Liberties Union, the National Council of Churches, and the British Guantánamo Human Rights Commission, founded and substantially funded by actors Vanessa and Corin Redgrave. "This is not the sort of case you walk away from once you have started," he said.

Docke knew his client had no recourse to U.S. courts and

could be held in Guantánamo indefinitely. A World War II Supreme Court decision, *Johnson v. Eisentrager*, had established that enemy combatants held and tried outside the United States have no right to habeas corpus. Guantánamo, although permanently leased by the United States and absent of any suggestion of Cuban civil or military authority, was, by the law and logic of the Bush-Cheney administration, outside the United States. In April 2004, the Supreme Court was scheduled to hear the case that challenged *Eisentrager*. Docke traveled to Washington with Rabiya Kurnaz. As justices heard the arguments of the lawyers representing Shafiq Rasul and other Guantánamo detainees, Rabiya Kurnaz stood on the steps of the Supreme Court building, holding a large photo of her son and speaking to reporters. The Supreme Court heard two Guantánamo cases that week: the *Rasul* case, which would provide habeas rights for foreign detainees, and the *Hamdi* case, which challenged the president's right to declare an American citizen an enemy combatant and hold him indefinitely in a military prison.

In June 2004, by a six to three vote, the Supreme Court ruled in favor of the detainees in *Shafiq Rasul, et al., Petitioners v. Bush, President of the United States, et al.* (The justices also ruled against the president in *Hamdi v. Rumsfeld.*) The doors of American courtrooms were now open to Murat Kurnaz and other detainees at Guantánamo. In a concurring opinion, Justice Anthony Kennedy addressed Donald Rumsfeld and Dick Cheney's transparent fiction that the American base at Guantánamo was part of the sovereign nation of Cuba:

> Guantánamo Bay is in every practical respect a United States territory and it is one far removed from any hostilities. . . . In a formal sense, the United States leases the Bay; the 1903 lease agreement states that Cuba retains "ultimate sovereignty" over it. . . . At the same time, this lease is no ordinary lease. Its

> term is indefinite and at the discretion of the United States. What matters is the unchallenged and indefinite control that the United States has long executed over Guantánamo Bay. From a practical perspective the indefinite lease of Guantánamo Bay has produced a place that belongs to the United States, extending the "implied protection" of the United States to it.

"We immediately filed in district court in Washington," Docke said. The Center for Constitutional Rights recruited Baher Azmy, a law professor at Seton Hall Law School in New Jersey, to represent Kurnaz. Azmy flew to Guantánamo.

"When he came to talk to me, I didn't believe him," Kurnaz said of his lawyer's first visit to the prison camp in Cuba. "I thought it was a trick to get information. I told him to go get me some coffee [to prove that he had some authority]. Then he gave me a letter from my mother."

In October 2004, the two lawyers finally got Kurnaz's file. "I was shocked when I read through it," Docke said. "There was nothing in the file that justified a yearlong detention. Nothing that justified holding Murat."

> *The interrogation process itself provides an opportunity for an individual to explain that this has all been a mistake.*
>
> —U.S. solicitor general PAUL CLEMENT

At Guantánamo, Murat Kurnaz was subjected to hundreds of days of interrogation. He was repeatedly asked if he knew Mohammad Atta, one of the 9/11 hijackers. He was asked what he did with the money he withdrew from the bank in Bremen before he left. He was asked why he sold his cell phone before leaving Germany. He was asked about his imam at the Abu Bakr Mosque. He was asked if he hated nonbelievers. He was asked if he hated his mother. His interrogators revealed their command of much of the detail of his personal life in Bremen and asked him about friends in Germany. He was frequently asked about his association with al-Qaeda.

Paul Clement was an assistant U.S. solicitor general when he told Supreme Court justice Ruth Bader Ginsburg that detainees don't need access to federal courts because the interrogations at Guantánamo provide an opportunity to explain that their detention was a mistake. One of the brightest and most accomplished lawyers in the country, who had once worked at Kirkland & Ellis, home to Whitewater prosecutor Kenneth Starr, Paul Clement knows better.

Kurnaz's case brings into high relief the perniciousness of Solicitor Clement's argument, which would be laughable if it weren't the sort of courthouse dishonesty that rises to the level of criminality. The interrogation process is designed to extract information, not to provide detainees the opportunity to exonerate themselves.

During a protracted interrogation regimen that Guantánamo guards called "Operation Sandman," Kurnaz was subjected to sleep deprivation for a month and intermittently interrogated for hours, sometimes for more than a full day. "I remember that nothing anybody said made sense to me," Kurnaz said. Defendants rarely rectify prosecutors' errors under such circumstances.

An exhibit admitted as evidence in one of the federal court cases challenging the constitutionality of the Guantánamo detentions includes a more detailed description of the interrogation process that Paul Clement claims provides detainees the opportunity to clear their names and address prosecutorial errors.

An FBI agent writes:

> On a couple of occassions [*sic*], I entered interview rooms to find a detainee chained hand and foot in a fetal position to the floor, with no chair, food or water. Most times they had uri-

> nated or defacated [*sic*] on themselves, and had been left there for 18–24 hours or more. On one occassion [*sic*], the air conditioning had been turned down so far and the temperature was so cold in the room, that the barefooted detainee was shaking with cold. When I asked the MPs what was going on, I was told that interrogators from the day prior had ordered this treatment, and the detainee was not to be moved. On another occassion [*sic*], the A/C had been turned off, making the temperature in the unventilated room probably over 100 degrees. The detainee was almost unconcious [*sic*] on the floor, with a pile of hair next to him. He had apparently been literally pulling his own hair out through the night. On another occassion [*sic*], not only was the temperature unbearably hot, but extremely loud rap music was being played in the room, and had been since the day before, with the detainee chained hand and foot in the fetal position on the tile floor.

Murat Kurnaz had been subjected to the hot-and-cold interrogation routine described by the FBI investigator. It failed to provide him the opportunity to correct the factual record. Yet in his case, the factual record, or "evidence" that kept him in prison for almost five years, was pretty thin.

Much of it was related not to him but to the friend he left at the airport when he left Germany in 2001. And it pertained to a terrorist act that occurred in 2003 while Kurnaz was sweating out life in Guantánamo. American intelligence had tracked Selcuk Bilgin to Turkey and described him as the "Elalananutus suicide bomber" who died when he blew up an Istanbul synagogue in November 2003.

It was a shaky foundation on which to build a case. The bombing occurred while Kurnaz was locked up in Guantánamo. Gokhan Elaltuntas, not Elalananutus, died when he detonated the truck he had loaded with explosives. Within days of the bombing, Turkish investigators used DNA to identify Elaltuntas and his accomplice, Mesut Cabuk. And Bernhard Docke had tracked down Selcuk Bilgin in Bremen to interview him exactly one year after the bombing in which American intelligence said he blew himself up in Turkey.

Selcuk Bilgin turned out to be a stand-up guy. "This I can say only: I heard the term Elalananutus for the first time on 22 October, 2004. Therefore, I knew nothing about this unknown person," Bilgin wrote in an affidavit Docke transcribed and translated. The report of Selcuk Bilgin's death in Turkey had been greatly exaggerated. The American intelligence that resulted in Murat Kurnaz's detention, torture and incarceration was as sloppy as the spelling of Elalananutus.

There was also documented proof that the Command Intelligence Task Force in Guantánamo had concluded Kurnaz's arrest and detention might have been a mistake. Kurnaz's American attorney had seen the evidence he believed would clear his client, but he couldn't discuss it in open court, or with Kurnaz, because it was in the classified section of the file. But Kurnaz's classified file was inadvertently declassified and obtained by *The Washington Post*. It revealed that not even the interrogators and analysts on the Guantánamo task force believed Kurnaz was guilty: "CITF had no definite link/evidence of detainee having an association with al Qaida or making any specific threat against the U.S.," one document read. "CITF is not aware of evidence that Kurnaz is or was a member of Al Quaeda [*sic*]." The statement that should have freed Murat Kurnaz had sat in his file since 2002.

Kurnaz's lawyer Azmy discovered that German intelligence officers had also interrogated Kurnaz in 2003 at Guantánamo and concluded he had not been associated with any suspect groups or individuals while he was in Germany. They even considered recruiting Kurnaz to work underground in the Muslim community in Bremen but decided he was so unsophisticated and unconnected that he would be of no use as a snitch.

Yet on September 30, 2004, a three-member military tribunal

had questioned Kurnaz. At the end of a hearing that took less than forty-five minutes, the tribunal reached its conclusion:

> By a preponderance of the evidence, that Detainee I is properly designated as an enemy combatant. . . .
>
> In particular, the Tribunal finds that this detainee is a member of al-Qaida.

In January 2005, Washington, D.C., federal district judge Joyce Hens Green heard Kurnaz's case, along with the cases of ten other detainees. Judge Green decided to review all the evidence, classified and unclassified. She found nothing that justified holding Murat Kurnaz. Among the hundreds of pages used to declare him a member of al-Qaeda, the one hot document included vague allegations made by one unidentified military officer. The judge was disturbed by the fact that Kurnaz, like other detainees, was never permitted to see or rebut the allegations that kept him in a cage in Guantánamo. She devoted seven pages of her seventy-five-page opinion to the government's case against Murat Kurnaz. "Even if all of the unclassified evidence were accepted as true, it alone would not form a constitutionally permissible basis for the indefinite detention of the petitioner," she wrote.

Judge Green's ruling wasn't enough to free Murat Kurnaz. Another D.C. district court judge, Bill Clinton appointee James Robertson, ruled as she did. But a third judge, sitting in the same courthouse, handed down a contradictory ruling. Richard Leon, a member of the right-wing Federalist Society appointed to the bench by George W. Bush in 2002, ruled that the tribunal process in Guantánamo was adequate and that detainees were not entitled to access federal courts. The government appealed, and Judge Green's opinion was stayed until an appeals court decided which opinion would stand.

Ten months after Judge Green ruled that detainees could not be denied the right of habeas corpus, President Bush signed the

Military Commissions Act, which provided a new military tribunal process for detainees at Guantánamo. It included an amendment by South Carolina Republican senator Lindsey Graham that denied detainees the right to habeas corpus. The new law put the appeals of Kurnaz and other Guantánamo detainees on hold until cases worked their way through the new tribunal process back into the courts.

It was an election in Germany, and not Judge Green's ruling, that sent Kurnaz home. Angela Merkel had defeated Gerhard Schroeder, Europe's most vocal critic of George Bush's Iraq war. As Merkel was putting together a governing coalition, the German public was disturbed by reports of Germany's participation in the rendition process—extrajudicial kidnappings by which the CIA moves suspects into countries where torture is practiced or tolerated. Docke and Azmy seized the moment and began a public relations campaign on behalf of Kurnaz.

"We told all of Germany that German agents had visited him and interrogated him in Guantánamo," Docke said. "Germans began to ask what their government had to do with keeping Murat Kurnaz in jail." New reports that German agents had flown to Guantánamo were a lot bigger than just one bad-news day in Berlin. The German public has a sensitive gag reflex regarding torture and indefinite detention. It was widely believed that because Schroeder had opposed the Iraq war, he would never allow German collaboration with American renditions or the detention program in Guantánamo. Schroeder had come from behind and won one election by running against Bush's war in Iraq, and he almost did it a second time in 2005, when he narrowly lost to Merkel. After Docke went public with Kurnaz's story, the German parliament began investigating allegations that the United States had offered to return Kurnaz but the "red-green" Schroeder government had said no—perhaps to keep the lid on reports about German interrogators working in Guantánamo.

A week before Christmas 2005, Docke wrote to Merkel, asking her to approach the U.S. government on behalf of his client. The chancellor responded in three days, then raised the issue with George Bush when she met with him in early 2006. The political planets were in alignment. Bush had been used as a Gerhard Schroeder campaign prop, and Bush's popularity among the German people was on a par with that of Saddam Hussein. The American president shrewdly decided on a gesture of support for the conservative German politician who had rid him of Schroeder. He told Merkel he would begin the process to free Murat Kurnaz. It would take six months to get Kurnaz out of Guantánamo, but Merkel left Washington with the promise that he would be freed.

For Kurnaz, there was one final degradation before the plane ride home. A week before he was returned to Germany, an escort squad walked him to an interrogation room, sat him in a chair, and shackled his hands and feet to a large ring on the floor. On a table in front of him was a telephone. A guard told Kurnaz to expect an important phone call. Kurnaz was left alone in the room for several hours. When the phone rang, he was unable to answer it, because he was so tightly shackled. He managed to move the table with his legs, knocking the receiver to the floor.

He leaned over and shouted into the receiver, then heard Baher Azmy's voice.

"Murat," he said. "You're being freed. You're going home."

POSTSCRIPT

Ten months after Murat Kurnaz was returned to Germany, the new tribunal system put in place by George Bush and Lindsey Graham began to fall apart. In June 2007, two Guantánamo tribunals ruled that two unlawful enemy combatants were not properly designated "unlawful." Both were enemy combatants, but the process for designating them "unlawful combatants" was unclear. Then an Army officer decided he had seen more than his conscience could bear. Lieutenant Colonel Stephen Abraham is an intelligence officer who had served on Combat Status Review Tribunals in Guantánamo. He had also been assigned to review the process of gathering evidence and preparing the prosecution's case against detainees. Abraham, a California corporate lawyer when he isn't an active duty reservist, submitted an affidavit in another Guantánamo case filed in a federal district court. (He is also the grandson of Holocaust survivors.)

Abraham described a process in which tribunals were rigged to ensure that detainees were declared "unlawful enemy combatants." Staff reviews of evidence to be used to convict detainees, he wrote, were often limited to checking grammar and spelling, rather than carefully vetting the quality of the intelligence. Behind those reports, Abraham found a system of gathering evidence that relied on junior officers with limited intelligence experience assembling material from "generic" sources that didn't relate to the detainee on trial. Most devastating was Abraham's account of the pressure brought to bear on members of the tribunals to deliver what were essentially guilty verdicts, which would justify indefinite detention.

Abraham recounted in detail a tribunal hearing in which he and two other officers ruled there was not sufficient evidence to declare the detainee an enemy combatant. Their commanding officer, a rear admiral, ordered Abraham to reopen the hearing and allow the prosecution to provide further evidence and argument.

Soon after the Abraham affidavit provided yet another bad-news day for Bush administration defenders of Guantánamo, the Supreme Court spoke to the detention issue. In a rare move that required the votes of five justices, the Court reversed its previously stated "wait and watch" position. There had been no petition for a new hearing on any particular case, and not since the 1940s had the court decided to examine a controversy absent a specific case. The justices announced that they would review the detention and trial process at Guantánamo when the court reconvened in fall 2007.

EIGHT

Terrorist Surveillance Program or Warrantless Wiretaps?

The right of the people to be secure in their persons, houses, papers, and effects, against unreasonable searches and seizures, shall not be violated, and no Warrants shall issue, but upon probable cause, supported by Oath or affirmation, and particularly describing the place to be searched, and the persons or things to be seized.

—Fourth Amendment to the United States Constitution

What can you do? If your government is going to do this stuff, they have the guns and they have the jails. At least we're in a democracy. You can file a lawsuit.

—plaintiff's attorney Tom Nelson

These are important, incredibly important issues, with constitutional dimensions, about the president's power to defend the nation from a terrorist attack.

—Department of Justice attorney Andrew Tannenbaum

This wasn't quite Watergate.

But there are similarities. Second-rate burglars. State secrets. An office complex overlooking a big American river. The political use of the courts and the Department of Justice to sustain a cover-up. And a corrupt administration.

Jonathan Norling was lying on the couch in his law office on a May morning in 2005. It was too early for the cleaning crew in the office complex situated just across the Willamette River from downtown Portland, Oregon. Yet a man wearing a familiar uniform was at the door. When he saw Norling on the couch, he left. Two months later, Norling was in the building late at night and ran into the same man in the same uniform—twice, again hanging around the door to his law office. Again the man fled.

"This person clearly wasn't a cleaning crew," Norling told a reporter at *The Oregonian.* "I know the cleaning crew. They have a cart, and this guy didn't have a cart. I've worked here for seven years and I've worked a lot of late nights. And I never experienced anything like that until Tom was working on this case."

Norling shared office space with his law partner, Tom Nelson. Nelson can't prove it, but the "cleaning crew" were probably federal agents, using sneak-and-peek provisions of the USA Patriot Act to break into the office. Nelson already knew something wasn't right. He would arrive in the morning and find that his computer had been shut down and rebooted, while no other computer or electrical appliance in the office had been turned off. Papers on his admittedly disorderly desk were left in odd places. Even the receptionist joked about night visitors. Nelson had written U.S. attorney Karin Immergut in September 2005, asking if she was aware of any federal surveillance. Immergut had reassured him that no search of his office had been authorized by the U.S. attorney's office in Portland.

Nelson moved his sensitive-case files to his cabin at the foot of Mount Hood. And someone broke in there, disabling the alarm. The technician who came out to repair the system couldn't explain what had happened.

In December, *New York Times* reporters Eric Lichtblau and James Risen broke a story about the National Security Agency's warrantless surveillance of electronic communication between subjects in the United States and suspicious contacts outside the country. "I wasn't aware of the significance of the documents until I read *The New York Times* and realized we had a smoking gun that proved the NSA had violated attorney-client privilege and the Fourth Amendment," Nelson said. (Never mind violating the Foreign Intelligence Surveillance Act.)

The "documents" Nelson refers to contained a surveillance log and transcript of warrantless intercepts of privileged communication between a client of his in Saudi Arabia and two lawyers in Washington, D.C. After the *Times* broke the story and President Bush made a speech admitting (if one is a stickler for the law) to a crime, Nelson prepared to file suit on behalf of his client, who he realized had been a subject of illegal surveillance. He also sent another letter to U.S. attorney Immergut, asking if she was aware of any surveillance targeting him. She assumed Nelson's complaints about clandestine searches referred to the NSA operation reported by the *Times.* That program, Immergut wrote, operates outside the Department of Justice. She had not been aware of it until she read about it in *The New York Times.*

Nelson wrote to the NSA, asking for a copy of his file, and was reassured that the agency had no file on him. He sent a second letter, and the agency hedged its response: "Rest assured that safeguards are in place to protect the civil liberties of U.S. citizens. However, because of the highly classified nature of the program, we can neither confirm nor deny the existence of records responsive to your request."

"In other words," Nelson said, "they weren't saying, 'We don't have a file on you.' They were saying, 'If we do, you are not going to get it.' "

Nelson had reason to suspect federal agents had been in his office. He had briefly represented Brandon Mayfield (see Chapter 5) after FBI agents spent days in Mayfield's suburban Portland home, downloading his computer files, photocopying his children's Spanish homework, and leaving telltale footprints on the carpets. Like Mayfield, Nelson was a convert to Islam, and he was acutely aware of the prosecutorial zeal with which the federal authorities were going at the Muslim community.

Nelson didn't have the document the government was after while the "cleaning crew" was tossing his office, though he was aware of its contents. But he obtained a copy after the *Times* story ran and returned it to the government in an indirect fashion: attached, under seal, to a lawsuit he filed on behalf of the client the NSA had targeted. It was such a "hot doc" that, at the government's request, the judge ordered it locked up in a SCIF—a sensitive compartmented information facility, of which there are two in the Northwest.

The document that had the feds on orange alert originally arrived in a large file delivered to Washington, D.C., lawyer Lynne Bernabei's mailbox on August 20, 2004. Bernabei was one of a team of lawyers representing the Al-Haramain Foundation. Al-Haramain was at the time Saudi Arabia's largest domestic and international charity, promoting conservative Wahhabi Islamic values and education. It had an annual budget of $30 to $80 million and offices in fifty countries, including one in Ashland, Oregon. Because the document marked "Top Secret" had been sent to her by the Treasury Department, Bernabei assumed it had been declassified. It was a log and transcripts of telephone conversations between two other Al-Haramain attorneys in Washington, Wendell Belew and Asim Ghafoor, and an agent of the

Saudi-based charitable foundation, Soliman al-Buthi, in Saudi Arabia.

The leaked document not only compromised the government's warrantless wiretapping program, which violated the Foreign Intelligence Surveillance Act. It also revealed that the staff at the NSA and the Treasury Department's Office of Foreign Assets Control were bunglers who mailed out a top-secret document that ultimately ended up in the hands of a Saudi subject the feds had listed as a "Specially Designated Global Terrorist"—and also in the hands of a naturalized American citizen from Iran, believed to be living in the United Arab Emirates. Not the sort of behavior that we expect in agencies at the forefront of our Global War on Terror.

It was predictable that Soliman al-Buthi and Perouz Sedaghaty would get copies of the NSA paperwork. Al-Buthi was the subject of the surveillance recorded in the leaked document. He is a Saudi government official who worked as a volunteer for Al-Haramain and was on the Oregon office's board of directors. Sedaghaty was the director of Al-Haramain's Oregon office. When the feds inadvertently mailed the file to Bernabei, she forwarded the material to her clients. The Office of Foreign Assets Control had allowed her one business day, rather than the two weeks she'd requested, to respond to what they'd sent her. So she immediately distributed the file, including the top-secret document, to all parties.

So, long before U.S. district judge Garr M. King ordered the NSA document locked in a secure vault, copies of it were floating around Riyadh. And possibly the UAE. Two of the countries in which the bad guys are plotting our violent destruction, because as G. W. Bush says, they "hate us because we're free."

If bungling bureaucrats at NSA and the OFAC created a security crisis by mailing out classified paperwork, the FBI agents called in to secure the document don't come off as the most nimble foot soldiers in the War on Terror either. In October—two months after the inadvertent leak—an FBI agent showed up at Wendell Belew's law office in Washington. The agent demanded the "top-secret" material that Bernabei had sent Belew. Then—stealing a page from sitcom special agent Maxwell Smart—the FBI agent warned Belew that he'd better not try to remember anything he'd read in the classified document.

The damage control was a little late.

Belew had sent a copy to *The Washington Post*'s David Ottaway, who was writing about the process the Treasury Department used to designate Specially Designated Global Terrorists. When the FBI requested it, Ottaway returned his copy of the document, as did the other lawyers who had received copies. It's safe to assume that all of them tried not to remember what they'd read. But one copy of the classified document remained in the files of Soliman al-Buthi in Saudi Arabia. And another had been sent to Perouz Sedaghaty, who the government assumed was in the UAE or Iran. Al-Buthi presumably provided the copy that Nelson filed with the lawsuit.

A brief recap.

Months before the *Times* broke the story about the surveillance program that Vice President Dick Cheney considered one of the "crown jewels" of American intelligence, the NSA sent a copy of the "top-secret" transcript to the Office of Foreign Assets Control. The OFAC mailed it to the attorneys representing the suspected foreign terrorists under surveillance. The attorneys sent copies to their clients in the Middle East, one a Specially Designated Global Terrorist. And to *The Washington Post* and others on the legal team. Two months later, the FBI sent agents out to retrieve the original and all the copies—and to order each recipient not to remember what he or she had read. No FBI agent went to Saudi Arabia to seize Soliman al-Buthi's copy and sequester his memory. If they knew where Perouz Sedaghaty was lying low, they didn't attempt to contact him either.

It was a stunning failure for the government.

And a critically important piece of evidence for the plaintiffs.

Lawyers, civil libertarians, and members of Congress can protest and hold hearings about the NSA surveillance program operating outside the law enacted in 1978 to regulate it. But a plaintiff was needed in order to get the program in front of a federal judge who could rule on its legality. A plaintiff, by definition, is someone who was affected or harmed. The American Civil Liberties Union and a group of scholars and journalists had in fact already filed suit in federal court in Detroit, where district judge Anna Diggs Taylor ruled the Terrorist Surveillance Program violated the "Separation of Powers doctrine, the Administrative Procedures Act, the First and Fourth Amendments to the United States Constitution and the FISA." But her decision was overturned by the Sixth Circuit Court of Appeals in July 2007, because the plaintiffs had "not shown that they were actually the target of, or subject to, the NSA's surveillance."

Al-Haramain was a different story. "We have proof that our clients were subjects of illegal surveillance," Tom Nelson said. "We also have proof that the government used what they learned about our clients to designate them. Otherwise, the documents wouldn't have been in that file."

The National Security Agency's Keystone Kop paper chase would be funny if the legal issues that set it in motion were not so disturbing—perhaps even alien to American justice. The USA Patriot Act, passed six weeks after the 9/11 terrorist attacks, gives the executive branch broad, unchecked power in many arenas—including the authority to designate any individual or group a terrorist or terrorist organization. It also includes provisions that allow the federal government to shut down charities and other nongovernmental organizations suspected to be conduits for moving money to terrorists.

Like many of the provisions of the Patriot Act, the power to "designate" marries the best intentions to the worst process. When the *Post*'s David Ottaway looked into how the federal government goes about designating charitable organizations, he found the government freezing the funds of suspect organizations at the beginning of an investigation, essentially a death sentence for the charities. Then the Office of Foreign Assets Control would follow up with an official designation that would close the deal, permanently putting the groups out of business. Charities could appeal in federal district court, but the government's cases are based on classified material the appellants cannot see, so it is rare that the terrorist designation is lifted. The process is flawed in other ways as well. Though the Treasury Department is authorized to designate a group or person as a "global terrorist," there is no legal definition of that term. Nor is there any established procedure to get off the list.

"If the category has no definition, then how would a group who challenges the definition know what it is?" Georgetown Law Center professor David Cole asked the *Post*. "It is whatever the government says it is."

Al-Haramain of Oregon was shut down because Soliman al-Buthi took $130,000 in traveler's checks and a $21,000 cashier's check out of the United States without declaring them. Al-Buthi didn't deny taking the money out of the country. It had been donated to Al-Haramain by an Egyptian physician who stipulated it be used in a relief effort for refugees in Chechnya, where the Russian Army was engaged in widespread human rights abuses in the brutal suppression of a separatist movement.

"Soliman didn't hide anything," Nelson said. "He walked into a bank, showed a Saudi passport, and withdrew money he said he was taking out of the country." When al-Buthi purchased his traveler's checks, in March 2000, an Arab withdrawing a large amount of money from a U.S. bank wasn't immediate cause for a teller to press the silent alarm button. What al-Buthi did, Nelson argued, was open and transparent, with money going from a bank in Ashland, Oregon, to a bank in Riyadh, Saudi Arabia. When FBI agents tracked down the cashier's check, it had "Donations for Chichania [*sic*] Refugees" written on it. Al-Buthi did, however, fail to declare the funds when he left the United States.

Nine months later, Perouz Sedaghaty (whose Anglicized name is Pete Seda) made an accounting entry designating the $151,000 drawn from Al-Haramain's account as funds applied to the purchase of a mosque in Missouri. On the financial report that charitable nonprofits are required to file with the IRS, Sedaghaty's account incorrectly entered the Chechen donation as funds applied toward the Missouri mosque. FBI agents reviewed Al-Haramain's financial statements and determined that the money had actually been sent to Chechnya.

It was careless but not criminal, Nelson said. The sort of thing for which companies, nonprofits, and individuals are usually charged and fined or stripped of their nonprofit classification. Yet the expatriation of $151,000 that had been sent to Oregon from Egypt with specific instructions to spend it on Chechen relief, and the incorrect or dishonest accounting entry that followed, was sufficient justification for the Office of Foreign Assets Control to freeze all of Al-Haramain's U.S. assets and begin an investigation in February 2004. In September 2004, the OFAC designated Al-Haramain Oregon a terrorist organization and al-Buthi a "global terrorist." The organization's bank accounts were seized and its real property auctioned off. In February 2005, both men and Al-Haramain Oregon were indicted on three counts, for conspiring to defraud the U.S. government and sending money to Chechnya.

Chechnya is old news that most Americans have long forgotten. But when al-Buthi withdrew $151,000 to send there, the Russian Army was engaged in its brutal campaign to put down the

Chechen separatists. The mostly Muslim insurgents in the former Soviet state were capable of acts of great brutality. But the Russian Army, initially under Boris Yeltsin and later under the heavier hand of Vladimir Putin, was the villain. Cities and villages were bombed, mass executions spread fear, and rape was widely used as an instrument of war—brutal in any culture but particularly effective (and devastating) in traditional Muslim communities, where feminine virtue and modesty are cultural imperatives. The Russians let slip the dogs of war, and Muslim charities and individuals around the world responded, funding relief efforts and in some circumstances providing funds to the separatists. The financial watchdogs of war in the United States, Great Britain, and most of Europe winked and nodded as Muslim donors funded humanitarian relief efforts in communities savaged by Putin's army.

The terrorist attacks on the United States focused the government's attention on the international movement of money. After 9/11, the FBI, CIA, and Treasury Department took a harder look at the financing of terrorism and found that some money used to finance international terrorism had been moved through Muslim charities, particularly outside the United States, and that Saudi Arabia had been a source and nexus of much of that funding. Choking off Muslim funding became unofficial U.S. policy.

Al-Buthi and Sedaghaty faced a 9/11 prosecution on a Chechnya rap.

The United States pressured the Saudis into shutting down the big Al-Haramain operation in Riyadh. With up to $80 million a year moving through it, some money that ended up in its foreign offices clearly found its way into terrorist bank accounts. Nelson said he can't vouch for Al-Haramain's fifty branches. But his guys, he said, are clean. He also said that American intelligence regarding Muslim charities at home and abroad had been sloppy and at times dishonest. Nelson points to the prosecution of the Holy Land Foundation, and Laid Saidi's extraordinary rendition and imprisonment in Afghanistan, are two examples of investigations gone bad—in Saidi's case, very bad.

The Holy Land Foundation for Relief and Development was the largest Muslim charity in the United States when its assets were seized, in December 2001. Seven of its officials were charged with funding the Palestine-based group Hamas. But odd things began to happen in the courtroom in Dallas. In particular, wiretap summaries of Holy Land Foundation phones, which were presented as evidence in court, didn't match the actual classified transcripts that one of the defendants somehow obtained. One of the summaries included virulent anti-Semitic and anti-Israel comments that even had Jesus Christ calling "Jews and their high priests the sons of snakes and demons," though no such language was found in the actual transcripts. Frustrated because they were unable to see the classified evidence the prosecution was using against their clients, attorneys representing the Holy Land Foundation asked Judge A. Joe Fish to declassify all the wiretap transcripts. Lawyers for the government protested that the declassification would gravely harm national security.

Laid Saidi never made it into a courtroom. Saidi is an Algerian and was the director of Al-Haramain's office in Tanzania when he disappeared in 2003. Tanzanian police had arrested him and escorted him to the border of Malawi. There they turned him over to Malawian police, who delivered him to American agents, who prepared him for extraordinary rendition—the Bush administration's signature kidnapping and extradition to a country where torture is tolerated. Saidi was blindfolded, his clothes were cut off, he was photographed, and his eyes were covered with tape. Someone inserted a plug in his anus and put a disposable diaper on him, then dressed him and loaded him on an airplane. He would spend fourteen months in a secret U.S. prison in Afghanistan, regularly interrogated about plans to purchase "airplanes," one of the key words intelligence officers began to look for after the airplane attacks of 9/11. Saidi finally got to listen to the audiotape of the transcribed conversation that had landed him in a CIA "black site." In a phone call to his brother-in-law in Kenya, he was mixing English and Arabic to make the English word "tire" plural by adding the Arabic "at" to the end of it. The party transcribing his wiretapped conversation wrote "tayarat"—Arabic for "airplanes." The on-site translator at the prison recognized the error. Saidi, who had been buying tires, was delivered into the hands of American torturers on a simple translation error.

The Holy Land Foundation might have been moving money to Hamas, but the prosecution ought to have been bound by the rules of evidence to prove that. Laid Saidi's treatment was a violation of human rights law, even if his abductors ultimately proved he was carrying a false passport. Once his captors (and torturers) got their translation straightened out, they returned him home to Algeria. When *New York Times* reporters Craig S. Smith and Souad Mekhennet questioned a CIA spokesman about Saidi's abduction and imprisonment, he didn't have much to say—except that the agency doesn't "comment publicly on these kinds of allegations . . . and does not condone torture."

Tom Nelson sees these (and other) cases as cautionary tales regarding good-faith prosecution and the quality of evidence the government is willing to use (or even fabricate) when bringing charges against Muslims.

The American public will forget the bit players in the Alberto Gonzales U.S. attorney scandal that compromised the integrity of the entire Department of Justice in the spring of 2007, including Gonzales himself, a political appointee for whom lickspittle is almost too generous a description.

James Comey was unforgettable. Ramrod straight and unflinching in the witness chair, he reminded the American public what public service truly means.

Comey, formerly the number two man at Justice under Attorney General John Ashcroft, told a riveting story of a late-night ride to George Washington University Hospital, where Ashcroft was critically ill. With sirens wailing and warning lights flashing, Comey and his security detail were in a race with Alberto Gonzales, who was then Bush's White House counsel, and White House chief of staff Andrew Card, who accompanied Gonzales.

Speaking to the Senate Judiciary Committee, Comey described the March 10, 2004, visit to Ashcroft's bedside as "probably the most difficult night of [his] professional life." Comey "ran up, literally ran up the stairs with [his] security detail." Behaving more like jackals than public officials, Gonzales and Card raced into the hospital room with an envelope. Comey had to stand at the attorney general's bedside to defend him from his other two visitors, who demanded that Ashcroft sign off on a program that Comey, designated acting attorney general while his boss was incapacitated, had already refused to reauthorize. The one-minute exchange that followed might have been John Ashcroft's finest hour:

"And Attorney General Ashcroft then stunned me," Comey recounted. "He lifted his head off the pillow and in very strong terms expressed his view of the matter, rich in both substance and fact, which stunned me—drawn from the hour-long meeting we'd had a week earlier—and in very strong terms expressed himself, and then laid his head back down on the pillow, seemed spent, and said to them, 'But that doesn't matter, because I'm not the attorney general.' "

Comey wouldn't describe in his testimony the secret program Gonzales and Card wanted Ashcroft to approve. It was, in fact, the NSA's warrantless surveillance program, or some part of it, which the policy shop at the White House designated the "Terrorist Surveillance Program."

The Foreign Intelligence Surveillance Act of 1978 was one of the reforms recommended by the Church Committee. Chaired by

Idaho senator Frank Church, the committee first investigated then proposed reforms to address executive branch abuse of intelligence and covert military operations in the years before the Watergate scandal. FISA was passed to place the surveillance programs under control of the federal courts. Under the law, a president, attorney general, or CIA director is required to go to a FISA court and get a "secret warrant" before putting an "American person" under surveillance. When it was passed, the law provided a twenty-four-hour grace period for emergencies, allowing the secret surveillance to be approved by the court one day after it was initiated. In 2001, the Patriot Act extended that time, allowing the NSA to request a warrant seventy-two hours after the surveillance begins. The FISA court almost always accommodated requests for warrants. From the time the bill was signed into law in 1978 until 2004, there had been 14,000 applications. Of which 13,995 were granted.

Yet the Bush administration bypassed all that and decided to go warrantless.

The program Bush and Cheney were running on their own doesn't involve a guy from your local phone company shimmying up your telephone pole. Before FISA was signed into law by President Jimmy Carter, the late Senator Church warned of a surveillance program "so powerful that if turned around on the American people no American would have any privacy left, such [is] the capability to monitor everything. . . . It doesn't matter. There would be no place to hide. The technological capacity that the intelligence community has given the government could enable it to impose total tyranny."

That was the program FISA was passed into law in 1978 to regulate. By 2004, the NSA surveillance program was far more technologically sophisticated. According to what the public knows about it today, the surveillance system links supercomputers on some twenty military bases across the globe. The computers channel intelligence gathered by giant golf-ball-like radomes to orbiting satellites that direct the electronic information stream to Ford Meade, Maryland. The program is believed to intercept 3 billion communications per day: phone calls, Internet, e-mails, faxes, telexes, microwave permutations of words, phrases, pictures, voices, addresses, phone numbers.

That's what the Bush administration turned on the American people, without going before the FISA court to get warrants. And that's what Tom Nelson, a team of lawyers, and their plaintiffs in Oregon and Saudi Arabia set out to challenge in federal court.

The Indian parable of "The Blind Men and the Elephant" could serve as a metaphor for the hearing held in Judge Garr King's Portland, Oregon, courtroom at the end of August 2006. Eight lawyers, two of whom had seen the top-secret NSA document, engaged in a protracted debate about its critical importance to the case each side was trying to make. Lawyers defending the government resorted to the sword of Damocles they routinely use to defend secrecy: Osama bin Laden. In this instance, it was an Oregon mosque and Islamic center "directly linked to Osama bin Laden" and "with ties to al-Qaida"—claims that Judge King, who had read the top-secret document, rejected.

There was nothing extraordinary about the government's warnings about bin Laden and al-Qaeda, although Nelson calls them completely unfounded regarding Al-Haramain's Oregon operation and Soliman al-Buthi. Jon Eisenberg, another member of the legal team representing Al-Haramain, argued that the DOJ lawyers ought to be required to back up such claims made in open court with evidence.

Yet the lawyers flown in from Washington, D.C., to defend the Bush administration's surveillance policy presented no evidence. Their argument was straightforward: Judge King had to dismiss the lawsuit Al-Haramain had filed against the president and various officials responsible for the warrantless surveillance. Because the top-secret document "is necessary not only for plaintiffs to prove their case but for defendants to present a defense," and because the release or discussion of even a highly redacted version of the document would cause "exceptionally grave damage to the national security of the United States," everyone should shake hands and go home. It was that simple.

Caught in the act of flouting FISA and the Fourth Amendment, the lawyers defending the NSA offered up riddles as defense: "The allegations at issue here are whether plaintiffs were subject to surveillance, and they say the document shows that fact. And that very fact, whether or not they were, is a privileged fact."

One might have expected the judge to respond, "Put cats in the coffee and mice in the tea." Yet Judge King wasn't buying the Lewis Carroll logic. Central to the government's defense was the claim that the Terrorist Surveillance Program was so secret that to admit its existence would put national security at risk. As DOJ lawyer Andrew Tannenbaum advanced that argument, the judge stopped him.

"The TSP program has been the subject of substantial broad disclosures on the part of the Government," Judge King said. "They've aggressively defended the program. They've outlined the nature of the program. There is a forty-two-page white paper supporting the program. How can the very nature, the very subject matter of this case be secret?"

When Tannenbaum argued that reports in the media are not the same thing as official confirmation that a program exists, the judge stopped him again.

"But if the president makes a statement," Judge King asked, "isn't that official? If the attorney general makes a statement, isn't that official? Now if you have filed pleadings in this case in which statements are made on behalf of all of these defendants, can I treat that as official?"

Backed into a corner, the DOJ lawyer's answer was brief: "Yes."

Eisenberg pointed to the absurdity of the secrecy argument by telling the judge he feared the NSA would want to "erase Mr. Nelson's memory."

The Honorable Garr M. King, appointed to the bench by Bill Clinton in 1998, earned his law degree at the University of Utah College of Law in Salt Lake City, then got a doctor of jurisprudence at Lewis & Clark Law School in Portland. Not first in his class at Harvard, Yale, or the University of Chicago, but a judge who understands you don't need a weatherman to know which way the wind blows.

Americans learned in a big way on 9/11 that the world is a dangerous place and that there are people actively plotting and acting to do the country harm. For all the judge knew, Soliman al-Buthi might have been hunkered down in a cave with Osama that very afternoon. But in a constitutional republic governed by the rule of law, it should be incumbent on the government to prove that in an adversarial proceeding where al-Buthi's attorney can stand before a judge, look at the evidence, and defend his client. (In fact, as the case was moving through the federal courts, al-Buthi was the director of environmental enforcement for the municipality of Riyadh. In the summer of 2007, though designated a terrorist by the U.S. government, he was invited to be a special guest at a dinner hosted by the American embassy in Saudi Arabia.)

Soliman al-Buthi is prohibited by the Saudi government from traveling to the United States, because the government and the royal family (sometimes it's hard to tell the difference) don't want one of their civil servants walking into a prosecution with the deck stacked against him. Perouz Sedaghaty was out of the country when he was indicted in 2004 and hadn't returned by midsummer of 2007, though sources close to him say he will come back to the United States and address the charges spelled out in his 2004 indictment.

Tom Nelson, who made a career as a utilities regulation lawyer and would probably otherwise be retired and riding his motorcycle across the Great American West, has found a second career. Or, more correctly, a second career found him. "This stuff affects me in a visceral way," Nelson said. "In this case, the federal government broke the law. If they had a FISA warrant, they would have filed it with Judge King and that would have been the end of it. But they engaged in illegal surveillance. They violated attorney-client privilege. Then they took what they got and used it. They used it! They used it in a civil proceeding, and my client never had a chance to defend himself."

Nelson is one of a half dozen people who has read the NSA transcript of conversations between al-Buthi and his Washington attorneys. He sees in it "a false positive" that the Treasury Department used to designate his client a terrorist. He wants a day in court to make that argument.

Jon Eisenberg, a constitutional lawyer from San Francisco who is on the trial team with Tom Nelson, is addressing issues far larger than Soliman al-Buthi and Perouz Sedaghaty: government secrecy and, more important, the division of powers defined in the first two articles of the Constitution.

Eisenberg directed the judge to a specific passage in FISA: "An aggrieved person who has been subject to electronic surveillance in violation of FISA shall have a cause of action against any person who committed such a violation."

"Now if the government has the right to keep secret forever that there was a violation of FISA," Eisenberg asked the judge, "then what meaning does [that section of the law] have?" If an individual can't prove he was subject to illegal surveillance, how does he have a cause of action?

Eisenberg reminded the court that the Congress writes the laws and the executive implements them. The president, he said, could have gone to Congress after 9/11 and said, "FISA is obsolete. Get rid of it. Give us the power we need." Eisenberg reminded the court that Attorney General Gonzales was very frank about why he didn't ask Congress for the authority to "thumb FISA." Gonzales and Bush feared that Congress would say no. "So their solution was, do what they knew that Congress wouldn't let them do."

The case that bears the title *Al-Haramain Islamic Foundation, Inc. v. George W. Bush, President of the United States, et al.*, has been consolidated with other similar claims and moved to federal court in San Francisco.

Jon Eisenberg told Judge King he doesn't want to unveil any state secrets or lay bare the technical workings of NSA's surveillance program. "We're not looking to reveal classified documents. We want a decision on whether or not the president's warrantless wiretapping program is unlawful," Eisenberg said. "That's our goal here."

POSTSCRIPT

On August 15, Perouz Sedaghaty, aka Pete Seda, came home. He had provided U.S. attorney Chris Cardani his flight itinerary. Two FBI agents took him into custody before he reached the Portland airport terminal. On the same day, a three-judge appellate panel in San Francisco heard oral arguments on the illegal wiretapping suit filed by Seda, al-Haramain, and al-Buthi. The judges were skeptical and at times impatient with Department of Justice attorneys defending the NSA wiretapping program.

A week later Pete Seda appeared before Judge Thomas Coffin in Eugene with a request to be released on bond. Cardani said Seda was a flight risk and cited alleged terrorist funding by al-Haramain offices in India and Indonesia. After a full-day bond hearing that included expert and fact witnesses, the judge said he would issue a ruling in two weeks after Seda answered questions about his travel in the Middle East.

CONCLUSION

We write in the first person plural because, though one of us left this project at the end of January 2007, it remained, until the final period was put in the proper place by our fabulous production editor, Beth Pearson, a collaborative endeavor involving both of us. Together we planned and revised chapters, abandoned dead ends, fretted over the Bush administration's contempt for human life, human rights, the rule of law, our Constitution, and the idea of a nation as commonweal in which we all have a stake.

We also argued over sentence length.

Yet we're wildly optimistic that the state of our republic will improve. The healing of our very sick body politic—and the restoration of constitutional government—began the day after the 2006 elections.

Our optimism is informed not so much by our stewards of the public trust in Washington but by the workaday American heroes in Oregon, South Carolina, Colorado, Pennsylvania, New Jersey, New York, Texas . . . people from both political parties and people from no political party. The principled women and angry men who stand up to the bullies, bastards, and ideologues who have hijacked our government and came dangerously close to destroying a document created by colonial subjects resolved to re-create themselves as citizens of a constitutional democracy.

The fight ain't over. But it's the courage and intelligence of the men and women we encountered while working on this book, and the courage and skill of the lawyers who went to court with them, that limited the damage George W. Bush has done to our Constitution since he took the oath of office in January 2001. (Our reporting has disabused us of the common notion that the current programmatic assault on our constitutionally guaranteed civil liberties began only after the terrorist attacks of September 2001.)

If they belong to a profession held in lower regard than loan sharks, every lawyer we came to know while working on this book is a public good in his or her own right. While defending their clients, they're defending our Constitution. Some work for the American Civil Liberties Union, the Center for Constitutional Rights, Americans United for Separation of Church and State, the National Lawyers Guild, People For the American Way, and the oxymoronic Texas Civil Rights Project. Others have no institutional affiliation but, in the spirit of the late Maury Maverick, Jr., of San Antonio, can't seem to pass up a good fight when they see one.

Judges are lawyers, too. The Article III judiciary is the crown jewel of our democratic form of government: 875 judges, appointed for life and therefore completely insulated from political pressure. "For life" means George W. Bush's legacy on the federal bench will still be in place when George and Laura's twin daughters are sexagenarians playing croquet on the lawn at Kennebunkport. The harm Bush and Cheney have inflicted on the federal bench should keep us all awake at night. The country is still blessed with a (diminishing) number of federal judges who refuse to exchange our freedom for a false security. And just as a blind hog can find an acorn once in a while, George W. Bush can appoint a gem of a jurist, like Judge John E. Jones III, of the Middle District of Pennsylvania. But if you see something we don't in the current crop of white Republican men who would be president and are promising to keep fear alive, Guantánamo open, and the federal courts in the hands of the Federalist Society, please call. If we don't hear from you, we'll assume you're writing your checks, walking your blocks, and working the phone banks to elect the woman or man who will begin the hard work of cleaning up the mess the "loyal Bushies" will have left us after eight interminable years.

We recognize the dedicated public service of Republican senators Susan Collins and Olympia Snowe (and former senator Lincoln Chafee), who refused to drink the Kool-Aid with Dick Cheney. But we also know that none of them could compete with the flat-earthers who make the cut in today's Republican presidential primary. Our continued optimism is contingent on who ends up in the White House in January 2009. And in control of the Senate, where federal judges are confirmed. And in an American public that will continue to elect officials who recognize the Constitution as the document that created and defines our republic.

So we conclude our conclusion. Never hesitant to recycle a good line when we find one, we'll quote ourselves quoting Matthew Chapman. It was Matthew who reminded us of the democratic social evolution by which the best and the brightest in this country rise to the occasion to do the very best for the country. A British expat living in New York (and the great-great-grandson of Charles Darwin), Matthew was covering the Pennsylvania courtroom fight between eleven parents who sued to keep the Book of Genesis out of their kids' high school biology classroom and a radical religious school board that considered the Bible foundational science.

There was a dead silence by the time one of those parents concluded a witness-stand soliloquy that no one sitting in the courtroom that September afternoon in Harrisburg, Pennsylvania, will ever forget.

> There are a lot of people that don't care. But I care. It crosses my line. . . . There have been letters written about the plaintiffs. We've been called atheists, but we're not. I don't think it matters to the Court, but we're not. We're said to be intolerant of other views. Well, what am I supposed to tolerate? A small encroachment on my First Amendment rights? Well, I'm not going to. I think this is clear what these people have done. And it outrages me.

It was Matthew, sitting in the jury box where reporters were watching the trial, who turned to his American colleagues and said in a whisper, "You know, I think the people we're looking at here are the very best of your country."

Spot-on, as we say in Texas.

Raise hell.

Keep fightin'.

And don't forget to laugh once in a while.

ACKNOWLEDGMENTS

Three weeks before her death at the end of January 2007, Molly Ivins was bedfast, nearing the end of a protracted struggle with metastastic cancer, and I was flying to New Jersey to interview one of the subjects of this book. I assured her that I would tell her about the interview as soon as I returned to Austin. "No," she said firmly, "call me as soon as you finish the interview." This book was Molly's project, the Bill of Rights her great love, writing her life's mission. We worked together pitching the book to Random House, and then shaping, reporting, and revising chapters. Molly wasn't inclined to let go. Not even when I returned from New Jersey to find her in Seton Hospital in Austin, less than a week before she returned to her South Austin home to die. From her hospital bed, in a voice so soft it was almost inaudible, she explained how we could best tell the story of the Bush administration's program to quash the First Amendment free-speech rights of American citizens who dared to criticize the president. This was what she cared about. Her determination to stay in the game was remarkable.

To recognize one of the authors of a book in the book's acknowledgments is unusual. We were working in unusual circumstances. Molly was a rare and dedicated professional, who twice a week in more than three hundred newspapers reminded people that they were not alone even if their political views didn't square with what the administration was selling. Harder to acknowledge is the loss of a colleague, a generous friend, and a very courageous woman.

Betsy Moon, Molly's inimitable personal assistant and friend, held this book project together under the most difficult circumstances. Charlotte McCann, who spends most of her time as publisher of *The Texas Observer*, was an invaluable colleague, providing research, editing, and constructive criticism. Our agent, Dan Green, in New York, moved this book from a proposal to its current form, again guiding us through paper processes that most writers find daunting and providing invaluable editorial suggestions. In Hamburg, Jim Lacy made critical connections for us and Tine Müller provided translations of books and documents used that allowed us to tell Murat Kurnaz's story. At Random House, Dan Menaker started this project and Jonathan Jao saw it to completion. And as she has on all of our previous books with Random House, associate copy chief Beth Pearson turned a rough manuscript into a book. Jeanne Goka-Dubose provided support, as well as criticism and commonsense advice rooted in the reality-based culture.

SOURCE NOTES

CHAPTER ONE INDEPENDENCE DAY

American Civil Liberties Union. "Secret Service and White House Charged with Violating Free Speech Rights in ACLU Lawsuit," ACLU–West Virginia, press release, September 14, 2004.

Baur, Terri. Telephone interview by LD, January 5, 2007.

Cohen, Henry. *Freedom of Speech and the Press: Exceptions to the First Amendment.* Congressional Research Service Report for Congress, updated June 2, 2006.

Howards, Steven. Telephone interview by LD, January 23, 2007.

Jeffrey Rank and Nicole Rank, plaintiffs, v. Gregory J. Jenkins, Deputy Assistant to the President of the United States and Director of the White House Office of Presidential Advance; W. Ralph Basham, Director of the United States Secret Service; John Does 1–2; John Does 3–4, defendants. In the United States District Court for the Southern District of West Virginia (Complaint), September 14, 2004.

Johnson, Hans. "The Home Front," *In These Times,* October 25, 2004.

Lane, David. Telephone interview by LD, January 12, 2007.

Levy, Leonard W. *Original Intent and the Framer's Constitution* (Chicago: Ivan R. Dee, 1988).

Meadow, James B. "From Boyhood Protest to Taking on Cheney," *Rocky Mountain News*, October 21, 2006.

Niederer, Sue. Interview by LD, Pennington, New Jersey, January 16, 2007.

Peyton, Harvey. Telephone interview by LD, January 15, 2007.

Pitts, Lewis. Telephone interview by LD, March 5, 2007.

Rank, Jeff. Interview by LD, Houston, Texas, February 9, 2007.

Rank, Nicole. Interview by LD, Houston, Texas, February 9, 2007.

Sarche, Jon. "White House Officials Can Exclude Dissenters," Associated Press, April 16, 2005.

Savage, Charlie. "Post-9/11 Limits on Dissent Claimed," *The Boston Globe*, December 14, 2003.

Simonich, Milan. "Judge Clears Bush Opponent," *Pittsburgh Post-Gazette*, November 1, 2002.

Star Ledger (N.J.), death notice for Seth Dorvin, February 9, 2004.

Steven Howards v. Virgil D. (Gus) Reichle, Jr. United States District Court for the District of Colorado, (Original Complaint), October 3, 2006.

Stone, Geoffrey. *Perilous Times: The First Amendment in Wartime* (New York: W. W. Norton & Company, 2004).

Waters, Sharon. "Mother of GI Killed in Iraq Arrested in 'Chaotic' Scene," *Asbury Park Press* (N.J.), September 17, 2004.

CHAPTER TWO A ZONE OF THEIR OWN

ACORN, USAction, United for Peace and Justice, The National Organization for Women, plaintiffs, v. The City of Philadelphia, The Police Department of the City of Philadelphia, and the United States Secret Service of the Department of Homeland Security, defendants. United

States District Court for the Eastern District of Pennsylvania (Amended Complaint), September 23, 2003.

Bovard, James. "Free Speech Zone: The Administration Quarantines Dissent," *The American Conservative*, December 15, 2003.

Bursey, Brett. Telephone interview by LD, February 26, 2007.

Buskey, Nikki. "Arrested Protestors File Lawsuit," *The Daily Texan* (University of Texas at Austin), January 21, 2005.

"Charges Overturned Against Crawford Five," *The Lone Star Iconoclast* (Crawford, Tex.), July 14, 2004.

Cohen, Henry. *Freedom of Speech and the Press: Exceptions to the First Amendment.* Congressional Research Service Report for Congress, updated June 2, 2006.

Commonwealth of Pennsylvania, plaintiff, v. William R. Neel, defendant. Before District magistrate Shirley R. Trkula in and for Allegheny County, Pennsylvania (Transcript of Proceedings), October 31, 2002.

Cowan, Lee. "Silencing Voices of Dissent," *CBS Evening News*, December 4, 2003.

Hightower, Jim. "Bush Zones Go National," *The Nation*, August 16, 2004.

Hilden, Julie. "Penning Protestors: Are Police-Imposed 'Free Speech Zones' and Cages at Conventions Constitutional?," FindLaw, August 13, 2004, http://writ.news.findlaw.com/hilden/20040803.html.

Johnson, Kirk. "Man Sues Secret Service Agent over Arrest After Approaching Cheney," *The New York Times*, October 4, 2006.

Katz, Jonathan. "Thou Dost Protest Too Much," *Slate*, September 21, 2004.

Levy, Leonard W. *Original Intent and the Framer's Constitution* (Chicago: Ivan R. Dee, 1988).

Lichtblau, Eric. "FBI Scrutinizes Anti-War Rallies," *The New York Times*, November 23, 2003.

Lindoff, Dave. "How the Secret Service and the White House Keep Protesters *Safely* out of Bush's Sight—and off TV," *Salon*, October 16, 2003.

Milbank, Dana. "Secret Service Not Coddling Hecklers," *The Washington Post*, September 10, 2004.

"Political Intelligence: Bush League in Crawford," *The Texas Observer*, June 24, 2005.

Roberts, Diane, "Zoned Out," *The New Republic*, May 13, 2002.

Rothschild, Matthew. "McCarthyism Watch: Protests, Even Buttons, Verboten in Crawford," *The Progressive*, March 18, 2004.

Stanley, Dick. "Crawford Protest Policy Challenged in Lawsuit," *Austin-American Statesman*, June 17, 2003.

Thurmond, J. Strom, Jr. "As Court Ruled, Bursey's Free Speech Not Trampled," *The State* (Columbia, S.C.), January 12, 2004.

———. E-mail communication with LD, March 13, 2007.

United States of America v. Brett A. Bursey, United States District Court for the District of South Carolina (Transcript of Verdict Hearing), January 6, 2004.

United States of America v. Brett A. Bursey. United States District Court for the District of South Carolina (Affidavit of Virginia Sanders), May 3, 2004.

United States of America v. Brett A. Bursey. United States District Court for the District of South Carolina (Appellee's Brief), July 13, 2004.

United States of America v. Brett A. Bursey. United States District Court for the District of South Carolina (Defendant/Appellant Reply Brief), August 10, 2004.

United States of America v. Brett A. Bursey. United States District Court for the District of South Carolina (Defendant/Appellant's Brief: Standard of Review), October 24, 2004.

United States of America v. Brett A. Bursey. United States District Court of Appeals for the District of South Carolina (Opinion), July 25, 2005.

Vlajos, Kelly Beaucar. "New Patriot Act Provision Creates Tighter Barrier to Officials at Public Events," *Fox News*, January 31, 2006.

Zafiris, Ken. Interview by LD, Austin, Texas, March 2, 2007.

CHAPTER THREE: THE KIDS ARE ALRIGHT

"AG Threatens to Prosecute Media over Leaks," *Fox News*, May 27, 2006.

Bates, Stephen. "The Reporter's Privilege, Then and Now," (Research Paper R-23, the Joan Shorenstein Center on the Press, Politics, and Public Policy, John F. Kennedy School of Government, Harvard University, April 2000).

Branzburg v. Hayes. Majority Opinion, Supreme Court of the United States, June 29, 1972.

Branzburg v. Hayes. Concurring Opinion by Justice Lewis Powell, Supreme Court of the United States, June 29, 1972.

Branzburg v. Hayes. Dissenting Opinion by Justice William O. Douglas, Supreme Court of the United States, June 29, 1972.

The Charlie Rose Show, transcript, July 6, 2006.

Corrigan, Dan. "Bond Issue: Sen. Kit Bond's Secrecy Act Would Gag Journalists—Even Jail Them," *Columbia Journalism Review*, November 1, 2006.

Garbus, Martin. *On the Media*, National Public Radio, February 26, 2007.

———. Interview by LD, San Francisco, March 8, 2007.

———. Telephone interview by LD, March 15, 2007.

Goodman, Amy. *Democracy Now!*, February 12, 2007.

Gross, Terry. "PBS Correspondent Lowell Berger Discusses New 'Frontline' Documentary About Relationship Between White House and the Press," *Fresh Air*, February 12, 2007.

House Select Committee on Intelligence, hearing transcript, May 26, 2006.

In re Grand Jury Subpoena, Subpoenaed Party Joshua Wolf. United States District Court for the Northern District of California, (Transcript of Proceedings), February 1, 2006.

In re Grand Jury Subpoena, Subpoenaed Party Joshua Wolf. United States District Court for the Northern District of California (Notice of Motion and Motion to Stay and Quash Subpoena and Subpoena Decus Tecum, Supporting Declaration of Jose Luis Fuentes), February 16, 2006.

In re Grand Jury Subpoena, Subpoenaed Party Joshua Wolf. United States District Court for the Northern District of California (Subpoenaed Party's Answer to OSC Re: Contempt), July 17, 2006.

In re Grand Jury Subpoena, Subpoenaed Party Joshua Wolf. United States District Court for the Northern District of California (Brief of Amicus Curiae ACLU in Response to Joshua Wolf's Answer to OSC Re: Contempt), August 1, 2006.

In re Grand Jury Subpoena, Subpoenaed Party Joshua Wolf. United States District Court for the Northern District of California, dated February 1, 2006, United States Reply to Brief Amicus Curiae, August 1, 2006.

Joshua Wolf v. The United States of America, Brief of Amici Curiae, submitted by Reporters for Committee for Freedom of the Press, WIW Freedom to Write Fund, Society of Professional Journalists, California First Amendment Coalition, in the United States Court of Appeals for the Ninth Circuit, August 11, 2006.

Lichtblau, Eric, and James Risen. "Bank Data Is Sifted by U.S. in Secret to Block Terror," *The New York Times*, June 22, 2006.

McCollam, Douglas. "The End of Ambiguity," *Columbia Journalism Review*, July/August 2006.

"News Wars: A Special Four-Part Investigation on the Future of News," PBS *Frontline*, February 14–February 28, 2007.

Reporters and Federal Subpoenas, Reporters Committee for Freedom of the Press, June 12, 2007.

Rosen, Jeffrey. "Full Court Press," *The New Republic*, November 13, 2003.

Stone, Geoffrey. "Scared of Scoops," *The New York Times*, May 8, 2006.

Taylor, Stuart. "Leak Prosecutions: The Gathering Storm," *The National Journal*, February 25, 2006.

U.S. Department of Justice, Federal Bureau of Investigation, "International Terrorism *Matters*," internal memo, February 26, 2003.

United States Senate Select Committee on Intelligence, hearing transcript, February 2, 2006.

"When Must Journalists Reveal Their Sources?," *Business Wire*, October 27, 2005.

CHAPTER FOUR DARWIN ON TRIAL

"A Not So Intelligent Design: Bush Does Science a Disservice," editorial, *Philadelphia Daily News*, August 4, 2005.

Americans United for Separation of Church and State, "Monaghan's Ave Maria Repays U.S. College Aid," *AU Bulletin*, August 2, 2005.

Badkhen Anna, "Anti-evolution Teachings Gain Foothold in U.S. Schools: Evangelicals See Flaws in Darwinism," *San Francisco Chronicle*, November 30, 2003.

Baker, Peter, and Peter Slevin. "Bush Remarks on 'Intelligent Design' Theory Fuel Debate," *The Washington Post*, August 3, 2005.

Behe, Michael J. "Design for Living," *The New York Times*, January 7, 2005.

Bumiller, Elisabeth. "Bush Remarks Roil Debate over Teaching of Evolution," *The New York Times*, August 3, 2005.

Caldwell, Christopher. "Creationism's Sly Evolution," *Financial Times*, January 22, 2005.

Caruso, Lisa. "Catholic Conservatives' New Advocates," *The National Journal*, September 3, 2005.

"Intelligent Design Rears Its Head," *The Economist*, July 30, 2005.

Kauffman, Christina. "Dover Parents: Let's Go to Court." *The York* (Pa.) *Dispatch*, April 11, 2005.

———. "Dover OK's Buckingham's Resignation," *The York* (Pa.) *Dispatch*, August 2, 2005.

Lebo, Laurie, and Michelle Starr. "Teachers: Our Output Not Applied: Dover Science Teachers Testified That They Taught References to Intelligent Design," *York Daily Record/Sunday News*, October 7, 2005.

Mooney, Chris. "Darwin's Foes Can't Evolve," *The New Republic*, October 17, 2005.

Ridgeway, James. "Making Monkeys of Us," *The Village Voice*, August 16, 2005.

Rothschild, Eric. Interview by LD, Philadelphia, September 28, 2005.

———. Telephone interview by LD, January 12, 2006.

Roward, Rev. Edward. Response to author's question regarding the testimony of John F. Haught, Harrisburg, Pa. September 30, 2005.

Tammy Kitzmiller et al. v. Dover School District. United States District Court for the Middle District of Pennsylvania (Complaint), December 14, 2004.

Tammy Kitzmiller et al. v. Dover School District. United States District Court for the Middle District of Pennsylvania (Opposition to Defendant's Motion for Summary Judgment), August 8, 2005.

Tammy Kitzmiller et al. v. Dover School District. United States District Court for the Middle District of Pennsylvania (Memorandum Opinion, Judge John E. Jones III), December 20, 2005.

Tammy Kitzmiller et al. v. Dover School District. Depositions: Behe, Michael; Brown, Jeff; Brown, Carol; Bosnell, Alan; Buckingham, William; Cleaver, Jane; Nilsen, Richard; Peterman, Trudy; Spahr, Bertha; Yingling, Angie, 2005.

Thompson, Richard. Press conference, Harrisburg, Pa., September 26, 2005.

———. Response to questions from author, September 27, 2006.

Walczak, Witold. Telephone interview by LD, August 24, 2005.

———. Telephone interview by LD, November 27, 2006.

Worden, Amy. "Bad Frog to 'Intelligent Design': The Controversial ex–Pa. Liquor Board Chief Is Now U.S. Judge in the Closely Watched Trial," *The Philadelphia Inquirer*, October 16, 2005.

CHAPTER FIVE SNEAKING AND PEEKING

Brandon Mayfield, an individual; Mona Mayfield; an individual; et al. v. John Ashcroft, Attorney General of the United States of America; Richard K. Werder, an individual; Terry Green, an individual; et al. United States District Court for the District of Oregon (Original Complaint), October 4, 2004.

"Bush Administration's Law Enforcement Response to Terrorism," Council on Foreign Relations (debate transcript), March 19, 2003.

Callimachi, Rukmini. "Government Acknowledges Using Patriot Act in Mayfield Case," Associated Press, March 29, 2005.

Cohen, Stanley. Telephone interview by LD, April 13, 2005.

Conner, Amy Johnson. "OR Lawyer Wins $2M for False Arrest in Madrid Terrorist Bombing," *Lawyers USA*, January 1, 2007.

Crombie, Noelle. "Mayfield Recalls 'Dark Nights' as FBI Witness," *The Oregonian*, June 25, 2004.

———. "FBI Outreach to Muslims Comes Amid Interviews," *The Oregonian*, July 22, 2004.

———. "Famed Lawyer Will Represent Muslim in Bombing," *The Oregonian*, August 27, 2004.

Denson, Bryan. "Mayfield Likens His Ordeal to Orwellian Nightmare," *The Oregonian*, November 30, 2006.

"The Enemy Within: Liberty and Security," *The Economist*, October 9, 2004.

Egan, Timothy. "Terrorism Task Force Detains an American Without Charges," *The New York Times*, April 4, 2003.

Eggen, Dan. "Justice to Probe FBI Role in Lawyer's Arrest; Faulty Fingerprint Analysis Linked American to Madrid Terrorist Bombings," *The Washington Post*, September 14, 2004.

Federal Bureau of Investigation. Statement on Brandon Mayfield case, press release, May 24, 2004.

In re Federal Grand Jury Proceedings 03–01, Case No. 04–9071 MISC-CR, Order, In the United States District Court for the District of Oregon, September 20, 2004.

In re Mayfield. United States District Court District of Oregon (Transcript), May 6, 2004.

Isikoff, Michael. "An American Connection," *Newsweek*, May 17, 2004.

Kariye, Mohamed Abdirahman. Interview by LD, Portland, Oregon, March 22, 2005.

"Kariye the Latest Target in Portland Terror Investigation," Associated Press, August 13, 2003.

Kershaw, Sarah, and Eric Lichtblau. "Bomb Case Against Lawyer Is Rejected," *The New York Times*, May 25, 2004.

———. "Spain Had Doubts Before U.S. Held Lawyer in Blast," *The New York Times*, May 25, 2004.

Kershaw, Sarah, Eric Lichtblau, and Dale Fuchs. "Questions About Evidence in U.S. Arrest in Bombing," *The New York Times*, May 22, 2004.

Kershaw, Sarah, Eric Lichtblau, Dale Fuchs, and Lowell Bergman. "Spain and U.S. at Odds on Mistaken Terror Arrest," *The New York Times*, June 5, 2004.

Lichtblau, Eric, William K. Rashbaum, and Laura Mansnerus. "Hard Charger on Terror War's Legal Front—Michael Chertoff," *The New York Times*, January 12, 2005.

"Mayfield's Luck: Only 2 Weeks Under False Arrest," unsigned editorial, *Newsday* (N.Y.), May 30, 2004.

McRoberts, Flynn, Steve Mills, and Maurice Possley. "Forensics Under the Microscope: Unproven Techniques Sway Courts, Erode Justice," *Chicago Tribune*, October 17, 2004.

Murr, Andrew, Kevin Peraino, Anne Belli Gesalman, Mark Hosenball, and Sarah Downey, "Joining Jihad: They Had Guns, and Plans for Afghanistan. Busting a Would-be Cell," *Newsweek*, October 14, 2002.

Nelson, Thomas. Interview by LD, Portland, Oregon, March 19, 2005.

Norris, Michelle, "Portland, Oregon, and Its Relationship with the FBI's Anti-terror Effort," *All Things Considered*, National Public Radio, February 11, 2005.

Robben, Janine. "What Price Security? The War on Terror Comes Home to Oregon," *Oregon State Bar Bulletin*, July 2004.

Rose, Joseph. "Mayfields' Home Goes from Safe to Sinister," *The Oregonian*, December 1, 2006.

Stout, David. "Report Faults FBI's Fingerprint Scrutiny in Arrest of Lawyer," *The New York Times*, November 17, 2004.

Teitler, Stanley. Telephone interview by LD, April 5, 2004.

Tizon, Thomas Alex, Sebastian Rotella, and Richard B. Schmitt. "Critics Galvanized by Oregon Lawyer's Case," *Los Angeles Times*, May 22, 2004.

Toobin, Jeffrey. "Should We Be Worried About the New Antiterrorism Legislation?," *The New Yorker*, November 5, 2001.

Wax, Steve. Interview by LD, Portland, Oregon, January 15, 2004.

Werder, Richard K. "Affidavit of FBI Special Agent Richard K. Werder," *In re Grand Jury Material Witness Detention*, May 6, 2004.

Zaitz, Les. "Authorities Suspect a Portland Mosque and Its Leaders Were Behind a Conspiracy to Help the Taliban, a Federal Filing Shows," *The Oregonian*, August 23, 2003.

———. "FBI Case Against Oregon Lawyer Built on Blurry Fingerprint, Logic," *The Oregonian*, May 30, 2004.

CHAPTER SIX ROE V. DOE

American Civil Liberties Union. "National Securities Letters by the Numbers," press release, March 9, 2007.

Anonymous. "My National Security Letter Gag Order," unsigned op-ed by John Doe I, New York, *The Washington Post*, March 23, 2007.

Bailey, Barbara. Telephone interview by LD, May 12, 2007.

Bailey, Barbara, Peter Chase, George Christian, and Janet Nocek. Press conference, Hartford, Conn., May 30, 2006.

Beeson, Anne. Telephone interview by LD, May 3, 2007.

Caproni, Valerie. Transcript of Testimony before House Judiciary Committee, March 28, 2007, *Congressional Quarterly*.

Chase, Peter. Telephone interview by LD, May 1, 2003.

Christian, George. Telephone interview by LD, April 27, 2001.

Cowan, Alison Leigh. "Judges Question Patriot Act in Library and Internet Case," *The New York Times*, November 3, 2005.

———. "A Court Fight to Keep a Secret That's Long Been Revealed," *The New York Times*," November 18, 2005.

———. "Librarian Is Still John Doe, Despite Patriot Act Revision," *The New York Times*, March 21, 2006.

———. "Four Librarians Finally Break Silence in Records Case," *The New York Times*, May 31, 2006.

———. "U.S. Ends Yearlong Effort to Obtain Library Records Amid Secrecy in Connecticut," *The New York Times*, June 27, 2006.

Doyle, Charles. *National Intelligence Letters in Foreign Intelligence Investigations: Background and Recent Amendments*, CRS Report for Congress, Congressional Research Service, updated March 20, 2007.

Durbin, Dick. "Statement of U.S. Senator Dick Durbin Regarding Department of Justice Inspector General's Report on the Patriot Act," March 9, 2007.

Gellman, Barton. "The FBI's Secret Scrutiny: In Hunt for Terrorists, Bureau Examines Records of Ordinary Americans," *The Washington Post*, November 6, 2005.

Graves, Lisa. "Testimony of Lisa Graves, Deputy Director of the Center for National Securities Studies (submitted in writing)," House Select Intelligence Committee on Intelligence, March 27, 2007.

House Select Intelligence Committee. Hearing transcript, May 28, 2007.

"The Inspector General's Independent Report on the Federal Bureau of Investigation's Use of National Security Letters," House Judiciary Committee, transcript, Federal News Service, March 20, 2007.

Jaffer, Jameel. Telephone interview by LD, April 19, 2007.

John Doe et al. v. Alberto Gonzales, Attorney General, et al. On Application to Vacate Stay, Supreme Court of the United States, Justice Ruth Bader Ginsburg (Opinion), October 7, 2005.

John Doe, American Civil Liberties Union, American Civil Liberties Union Foundation, plaintiffs, v. John Ashcroft, in his official capacity as Attorney General of the United States; Robert Mueller, in his official capacity as Director of the Federal Bureau of Investigation; and Marion Bowman, in his official capacity as Senior Counsel to the Federal Bureau of Investigation, defendants. United States District Court Southern District of New York, Opinion, Decision, and Order, Victor Marrero, United States District Judge, September 28, 2004.

John Doe, American Civil Liberties Union, American Civil Liberties Union Foundation, plaintiffs, v. Alberto Gonzales, in his official capacity as Attorney General of the United States; Robert Mueller, in his official capacity as Director of the Federal Bureau of Investigation; Michael J. Wolf, in his official capacity as Special Agent in Charge, Federal Bureau of Investigation, defendants. (In the District Court for the District of Connecticut), Declaration of David W. Szady, August 31, 2005.

John Doe, American Civil Liberties Union, American Civil Liberties Union Foundation, plaintiffs, v. Alberto Gonzales, in his official capacity as Attorney General of the United States; Robert Mueller, in his official capacity as Director of the Federal Bureau of Investigation; Michael J. Wolf, in his official capacity as Special Agent in Charge, Federal Bureau of Investigation, defendants (In the District Court for the District of Connecticut), Declaration of George Christian, August 15, 2005.

John Doe, American Civil Liberties Union, American Civil Liberties Union Foundation, plaintiffs, v. Alberto Gonzales, in his official capacity as Attorney General of the United States; Robert Mueller, in his official capacity as Director of the Federal Bureau of Investigation; Michael J. Wolf, in his official capacity as Special Agent in Charge, Federal Bureau of Investigation, defendants (In the District Court for the District of Connecticut), Ruling on Plaintiffs Motion for Temporary Injunction, September 9, 2005.

John Doe I, John Doe II, American Civil Liberties Union, American Civil Liberties Union Foundation, plaintiffs, v. Alberto Gonzales, in his official capacity as Attorney General; Robert Mueller, in his official capacity of Director of the Federal Bureau of Investigation; Marion E. Bowman, in his official capacity as Senior Counsel of the Federal Bureau of Investigation; and John Roe, defendants (In the United States Court of Appeals for the Second Circuit), Per Curiam Opinion, May 23, 2006.

John Doe I, John Doe II, American Civil Liberties Union, American Civil Liberties Union Foundation, plaintiffs, v. Alberto Gonzales, in his official capacity as Attorney General; Robert Mueller, in his official capacity of Director of the Federal Bureau of Investigation; Marion E. Bowman, in his official capacity as Senior Counsel of the Federal Bureau of Investigation; and John Roe, defendants (In the United States Court of Appeals for the Second Circuit), Brief of Amici Curiae submitted by American Library Association, Freedom to Read Foundation, American Booksellers Foundation, and Association of American Publishers, October 3, 2005.

Leahy, Patrick. "Senate Judiciary Panel Probes FBI's Misuse of Patriot Act Powers," Federal News Service, March 21, 2007.

Leone, Richard C., and Greg Anrig, Jr. *Liberty Under Attack: Reclaiming Our Freedoms in an Age of Terror* (New York: PublicAffairs, 2007).

Library Connection, Inc.; American Civil Liberties Union; American Civil Liberties Union Foundation, plaintiffs, v. Alberto Gonzales, in his official capacity as Attorney General of the United States; Robert Mueller, in his official capacity as Director of the Federal Bureau of Investigation; Michael J. Wolf, in his official capacity as Special Agent in Charge, Federal Bureau of Investigation, defendants (In the District Court for the District of Connecticut), Declaration of Peter Chase. Civil Action No. 3:05cv1256 JCH. Sealed Case, August 9, 2005.

Mauro, Tony. "Justice Department's Independence 'Shattered,' Says Former DOJ Attorney," *Legal Times*, April 16, 2007.

"National Security Letter Matters," Federal Bureau of Investigation, Memo to All Field Offices: Synopsis: Provides Guidance on the preparation, approval, and service of National Security Letters [author name redacted], November 28, 2001.

Rosen, Jeffrey. "Who's Watching the FBI?," *The New Yorker*, April 15, 2007.

United States Department of Justice Office of the Inspector General. "A Review of the Federal Bureau of Investigation's Use of National Security Letters," March 2007.

United States Senate Judiciary Committee. Subcommittee on the Constitution, Civil Rights and Property Rights, transcript, Federal News Service, April 11, 2007.

Weiner, Lauren M. "Special Delivery: Where Do National Security Letters Fit into the Fourth Amendment?," *Fordham Urban Law Journal*, November 1, 2006.

Wolf, Michael J., Special Agent in Charge, Federal Bureau of Investigation, National Security Letter to Kenneth Sutton, Systems and Telecommunication Manager, Library Connection, Inc., May 19, 2005.

CHAPTER SEVEN Our Time in the Shadows

Abraham, Stephen. Declaration of Stephen Abraham, Lieutenant Colonel, United States Army, June 15, 2007, submitted as part of a reply to an opposition to a petition for rehearing in the case *Khaled A.F. Al Odah et al. v. United States et al.* (No. 06–1196 In the Supreme Court of the United States).

Administrative Review Board Hearing Transcripts, Correspondence, and Exhibits, for Detainee Murat Kurnaz, unclassified, U.S. Naval Base Guantánamo Bay, 2005.

Azmy, Baher. Telephone interview by LD, May 23, 2007.

Chesney, Robert. "Ruling Expands Judiciary's Role in Transfer of Terror Detainees," Washington Legal Foundation, *Legal Backgrounder*, August 26, 2005.

Davies, Frank. "A Year Later, Ruling Stalled for Guantánamo Inmates," *The Philadelphia Inquirer*, June 30, 2005.

Docke, Bernhard. Interview by LD, Bremen, Germany, June 13, 2007.

Fava, Claudio (Member of European Parliament). *Extraordinary Rendition in U.S Counterterrorism Policy: The Impact on Transatlantic Relations*, Report to the United States House Committee on Foreign Affairs Subcommittee on International Organizations, Human Rights, and Oversight Committee on Europe, April 17, 2007.

Faces of Guantánamo: Guantánamo's Many Wrongly Imprisoned, Center for Constitutional Rights, April 2007.

Fox, Ben. "Army Officer Says Gitmo Panels Flawed," Associated Press, June 22, 2007.

Gellman, Barton, and Jo Becker. "The Unseen Path to Cruelty," *The Washington Post*, June 25, 2007.

Grigg, William Norman. "Land of the Free? Under Legal Theories Currently Being Developed and Deployed, Any Individual Can Be Imprisoned, Tortured, or Even Executed on a Presidential Whim," *The New American*, April 3, 2006.

Hamdi et al. v. Rumsfeld, Secretary of Defense, et al. Declaration of Michael H. Mobbs, Special Advisor to the Under Secretary of Defense for Policy, July 24, 2002.

Hamdi et al. v. Rumsfeld, Secretary of Defense, et al. Supreme Court of the United States, Certiorari to the United States Court of Appeals for the Fourth Circuit, June 28, 2004.

Hemingway, Thomas L. "Wartime Detention of Enemy Combatants: What If There Were a War and No One Could Be Detained Without an Attorney?," *Denver Journal of International Law and Policy*, March 22, 2006.

In re Guantánamo Detainee Cases, Memorandum Opinion Denying in Part and Granting in Part Respondent's Motion to Dismiss of for Judgment as a Matter of Law, United States District Judge Joyce Hens Green, January 31, 2005.

Jost, Kenneth. "Fitting the Nine in a New Docket," *CQ Weekly*, June 24, 2005.

Kaufman, Sam. Interview by LD, December 31, 2005.

———. Telephone interview by LD, January 12, 2007.

Kurnaz, Murat. *Fünf Jahre Meines Lebens: Ein Bericht aus Guantánamo* (Berlin: Rowohlt, 2007).

———. Interview by LD, Bremen, Germany, June 13, 2007.

———. Interview by LD, Bremen, Germany, June 14, 2007.

———. Telephone interview by LD, Bremen, Germany, June 15, 2007.

Lander, Mark, Souad Mekhennet, and Victor Homola. "Freed German Detainee Questions His Country's Role," *The New York Times*, November 4, 2006.

Leonnig, Carol D. "Panel Ignored Evidence on Detainee; U.S. Military Intelligence, German Authorities Found No Ties to Terrorists," *The Washington Post*, March 27, 2005.

Lewis, Neil A. "U.S. Lawyer Is Questioned over Rights of Detainees," *The New York Times*, September 9, 2006.

"Memorandum for Alberto R. Gonzales, Counsel to the President [the torture memo]," United States Department of Justice, Office of Legal Counsel, August 1, 2002.

Moore, Jennifer. "Practicing What We Preach: Humane Treatment for Detainees in the War on Terror," *Denver Journal of International Law and Policy*, March 22, 2006.

Murat Kurnaz et al. v. George W. Bush, President of the United States, et al. United States District Court for the District of Columbia, Declaration of James S. Crisfield, Jr., August 15, 2004.

Nicola, Stefan, "Report from Guantánamo," United Press International, April 26, 2007.

Norwitz, Jeffrey H. "Defining Success at Guantánamo: By What Measure?," *Military Review*, July 1, 2005.

Rasul v. Bush, President of the United States, et al. Supreme Court of the United States, Certiorari to the United States Court of Appeals for the District of Columbia Circuit, June 28, 2004.

"A Timeline of Legal Developments at Guantánamo Bay," Knight Ridder Newspapers, June 10, 2006.

Toobin, Jeffrey. "Arlen Specter's About Face," *The New Yorker*, December 4, 2006.

United States Senate Judiciary Committee Hearing on Detainees, Panel I, transcript, Federal News Service, June 15, 2005.

"Update to Annex One of Second Periodic Report of United States to Committee Against Torture," United States Department of State. Submitted by the United States to the United Nations Committee Against Torture, October 21, 2005.

CHAPTER EIGHT TERRORIST SURVEILLANCE PROGRAMS OR WARRANTLESS WIRETAPS?

Abramson, Larry. "Government Won't Release NSA Information to Attorneys," *All Things Considered*, National Public Radio, March 30, 2006.

Al-Haramain Islamic Foundation, Inc., an Oregon Non-Profit Foundation; Wendel Belew, a U.S. Citizen and Attorney at Law; Asim Ghafoor, a U.S. Citizen and Attorney at Law v. George W. Bush, President of the United States; National Security Agency; Keith B. Alexander, its Director; et al. Opinion and Order, United States District Judge Garr B. King, December 7, 2006.

American Civil Liberties Union et al. v. National Security Agency et al. United States Court of Appeals for the Sixth District (Per Curiam Opinion), July 6, 2007.

Anderson, Colleen (Special Agent, Internal Revenue Service). Affidavit in Support of an Application for a Search Warrant, In re: 3380 S. Highway 99, Ashland, OR, 97520 (United States District Court of Oregon), August 2, 2005.

Bedan, Matt. "Echelon Effect: The Obsolescence of the U.S. Foreign Intelligence Legal Regime," *Federal Communications Law Journal*, March 2007.

Center for Constitutional Rights, Tina M. Foster, et al., v. George W. Bush, President of the United States, National Security Agency, et al. United States District Court, Southern District of New York, January 17, 2006.

Chang, Nancy, and Alan Kabat. "A Summary of Recent Court Rulings on Terrorism-Related Matters Having Civil Liberties Implications," Center for Constitutional Rights, September 11, 2003.

Comey, James B. United States Senate Judiciary Committee Hearing, "Preserving Prosecutorial Independence: Is the Department of Justice Politicizing the Hiring and Firing of U.S. Attorneys? Part IV," testimony, May 15, 2007.

Denson, Bryan. "Lawyer Thinks Office Was Searched in Secret," *The Oregonian*, March 21, 2006.

"Government Files Motion to Dismiss Case Against Al-Haramain Islamic Foundation, Inc., Because International Fugitives Have Not Been Apprehended," United States Attorney's Office, District of Oregon, press release, August 4, 2005.

Green, Ashbel. "Judge Nixes U.S. Bid for Secrecy in Oregon Suit," Knight Ridder/ Tribune Business News, April 26, 2006.

Krikorian, Greg. "False Quotes Rock Terror Trial; Federal Prosecutors Say They'll Probe a Botched Wiretap Summary," *Los Angeles Times*, February 28, 2007.

Leonnig, Carol D., and Mary Beth Sheridan. "Saudi Group Alleges Wiretapping by U.S.; Defunct Charity's Suit Details Eavesdropping," *The Washington Post*, March 2, 2006.

McCall, William. "Islamic Charity Director's Attorney Says Office Secretly Searched," Associated Press, March 22, 2006.

Miller, Steve. "The 'Mystery' of Al-Haramain in the Balkans," *The Washington Times*, September 14, 2003.

OMB Watch. "The USA Patriot Act and Its Impact on Non-Profit Organizations," OMB Watch, Washington, D.C., September 3, 2002.

Ottaway, David B. "Groups, U.S. Battle over 'Global Terrorist' Label." *The Washington Post*, November 14, 2004.

Ragavan, Chitra, Carol Hook, and Jill Konieczko. "Packing Heat: The White House Defends Its Warrantless Spying Program, but a Small Army of Lawyers Is Gunning to Shoot It Down," *U.S. News & World Report*, March 13, 2006.

Roth, John, Douglas Greenburg, and Serena B. Wille. *Monograph on Terrorist Financing Staff Report to the Commission*, National Commission on Terrorist Attacks upon the United States, Washington, D.C., 2004, http://purl.access.gpo.gov/GPO/LPS53198.

Singel, Ryan. "Top Secret: We're Wiretapping You," *Wired*, March 3, 2007.

Winer, Jonathan. United States Senate Committee on Governmental Affairs Hearing: "Terrorism Financing: Origination, Organization, and Prevention," Testimony: "Origins, Organization and Prevention of Terrorist Finance," July 31, 2003.

Zaitz, Les. "Fugitive Solimon al-Buthi Is Asked to Dine at U.S. Embassy Event in Saudi Arabia," *The Oregonian*, May 31, 2007.

———. "Al-Qaida Trail Tracked to Northwest," *The Oregonian*, May 13, 2002.

Zeller, Shawn. "Islamic Charities Await Their Day in Court, *CQ Weekly*, May 25, 2007.

INDEX

ABOUT THE AUTHORS

MOLLY IVINS, a three-time Pulitzer Prize finalist, began her career in journalism as the complaint department of the *Houston Chronicle*. She then went on to work for *The Texas Observer*, as co-editor, and *The New York Times*, as a political reporter and later as Rocky Mountain bureau chief. In 1982, she returned to Texas. Her column was syndicated in more than three hundred newspapers, and her freelance work appeared in *Esquire*, *The Atlantic Monthly*, *The New York Times Magazine*, *The Nation*, *Harper's*, and other publications. Her first book, *Molly Ivins Can't Say That, Can She?*, spent more than a year on the *New York Times* bestseller list. Her books with Lou Dubose on George W. Bush, *Shrub* and *Bushwhacked*, were also *New York Times* bestsellers. Molly Ivins died in January 2007.

LOU DUBOSE has written about Texas and national politics for thirty years. He was editor of *The Texas Observer* and politics editor for *The Austin Chronicle*, and he currently edits *The Washington Spectator*. He was co-author (with Molly Ivins) of *Shrub* and *Bushwhacked*. In 2003 he wrote (with *Texas Monthly* writer Jan Reid) *The Hammer: Tom DeLay, God, Money, and the Rise of the Republican Congress*. In 2006 he wrote (with *Texas Observer* editor Jake Bernstein) *Vice: Dick Cheney and the Hijacking of the American Presidency*.

ABOUT THE TYPE

The text of this book was set in Janson, a typeface designed in about 1690 by Nicholas Kis, a Hungarian living in Amsterdam, and for many years mistakenly attributed to the Dutch printer Anton Janson. In 1919 the matrices became the property of the Stempel Foundry in Frankfurt. It is an old-style book face of excellent clarity and sharpness. Janson serifs are concave and splayed; the contrast between thick and thin strokes is marked.